BY MORGAN PARKER

Who Put This Song On?

Magical Negro

There Are More Beautiful Things Than Beyoncé

Other People's Comfort Keeps Me Up at Night

You Get What You Pay For

**YOU
GET
WHAT
YOU
PAY
FOR**

YOU GET WHAT YOU PAY FOR

Essays

Morgan Parker

ONE WORLD
New York

Published in the United States by One World, an imprint of
Random House, a division of Penguin Random House LLC, New York.

ONE WORLD and colophon are registered trademarks of
Penguin Random House LLC.

Library of Congress Cataloging-in-Publication Data
Names: Parker, Morgan, author.
Title: You get what you pay for: essays / by Morgan Parker.
Description: First edition. | New York: One World, [2024] |
Identifiers: LCCN 2023033598 (print) | LCCN 2023033599 (ebook) |
ISBN 9780525511441 (hardback) | ISBN 9780525511458 (ebook)
Subjects: LCSH: African Americans—Psychology. | African Americans—Race
identity. | African Americans in popular culture. | United States—Race relations. |
Parker, Morgan. | Depression in women—United States.
Classification: LCC E185.625 .P357 2024 (print) | LCC E185.625 (ebook) |
DDC 305.896/073—dc23/eng/20231108
LC record available at https://lccn.loc.gov/2023033598
LC ebook record available at https://lccn.loc.gov/2023033599

Printed in the United States of America on acid-free paper

oneworldlit.com

9 8 7 6 5 4 3 2 1

First Edition

Contents

YOU
GET
WHAT
YOU
PAY
FOR

START
AT
THE
BEGINNING

The first thing you're supposed to do is introduce yourself. If people don't know who they're encountering, they won't know how to perform the encounter. At which tenor, in what pitch, with how much respect.

People are always saying "start at the beginning," which must be some sort of sick joke. We love linear narratives, the smooth waters of sequential order. But it's too clean.

I was early by weeks. The story goes that when she went into labor, my mom thought the waterbed broke. This was 1987. The story goes that my dad, still drunk on Tanqueray from Mom's office Christmas party, drove her to the hospital two towns over, where I proceeded to change my mind about this whole enterprise, and kept my mother in labor for double-digit hours, as my dad experienced what I can only imagine was the worst and weirdest hangover of his life. They cut me out, let me incubate for a few weeks, and when it was determined that I was fully formed, I got started. I was early and then late, hesitating at the door.

Ten days after my birth, Prozac made its first appearance in the United States of America. Just after my twelfth birthday, all the clocks would set back to zero. We were living in the "End Times," my teachers said. Everything was a sign: Y2K, Britney Spears, homosexuals, Marilyn Manson. Clearly the Earth was falling apart, and if the Rapture was nigh one thousand years ago, any day could be my last to prove myself worthy. On my eighth-grade picture day, a plane would crash into a building I'd never heard of in New York City, and we'd get the day off to pray. I'm pretty sure the United States has been at war for my entire life.

I belong to a particular subcategory of millennials who searched library card drawers to research a paper to write by hand in cursive, and who only got a Nokia phone in middle school for emergencies or rides home after play practice. For us, first there was slime and Spice Girls and Pogs (anecdotally, now flagged for spell check), and patriotism was Michael Jordan and Kerri Strug, and our president played the saxophone. There were devil worshippers in suburban parks at night and El Niño winds in the morning and razors in Halloween candy. There was so much money, frivolous money—speedboats and liposuction and shoes that lit up. Then, it was the end of the calendar as we knew it and maybe the end of the world. Then, it was the end of democracy, because of the Arabs, all of whom were terrorists, maybe; and patriotism was obligatory, and our president's abhorrent grammar mistakes filled daily quote calendars. There were celebrity sex tapes and school shootings and machine gun videogames. You could be famous for no reason, and everyone had computer rooms, and we replaced our after-school phone calls with Instant Messenger. Then there was no money, and people lost their houses, and we were still at war. The banks owned us, it turned out, and the whole thing had been about oil. A lot of people started doing oxy.

There was sin and there was terror, and in their negative space I sculpted a self.

The first autobiography in my personal archives dates back to roughly 2001, which may be due to puberty's corresponding to one's social sense of self; but it could also be said that my autobiography—preserving myself—became necessary in the face of *terror*, that my narrative began under the moon of terror. Within its cultural context. Also, it was written by a seventh grader.

"In so many words I will try to describe—or, better yet, explain—myself. This is something I have not yet tried and feel is a necessary challenge. I simply cannot be labeled—not as a girl, nor as a student, nor a writer. But I guess that is how I should begin."

People are always telling you where to start, which is, in actuality, just another way of telling you where you can go.

"Being a girl also ensures many stereotypes—at which I am glad to clear up I do not like hot pink. Another stereotype is that girls are ditzy and stupid. I am not a ditz. In fact, I am un-

*doubtedly ~~smart~~ intelligent. I hate to sound proud, but this is
an inescapable action in order to better explain myself to others.
Though there are many other stereotypes, I feel that my point
has been given and taken respectively."*

Start at the beginning. You have to laugh.

THE DEVELOPMENTAL STAGES OF THE NEGRO CHILD WILL VARY
depending upon several extenuating factors, the most significant of which is environment. Outside the family unit,
environment will include public or private education, economic and geographical demographics, and access to a mirror. Negro children are born again as Negro children in a
white world and achieve differing levels of awareness
thereof, at varying rates and to varying degrees: a mirror
stage in which the mirror reflects both yourself and somebody else's vision of you.

For several reasons, including the prevalence of the Bible
and white girls, even as a child I understood that there was
always a me I desperately needed to keep secret, dark patches
to tuck away under my public self; a performance that sometimes required rising to the occasion of myself, and with
each occasion the dark parts dug deeper into a sinking feeling. The protective measure of hiding the whole truth of
myself and my mind: sharpening, sharpening.

Becoming aware of one's identity, not to mention making sense of it, is not an uncomplicated or straightforward
process—not when there are so many layers of a self to understand, so many lenses to see through, so much written on your

body that only others can read. With double consciousness—seeing oneself with two sets of eyes and their accompanying assumptions—comes a double vision, doubled self-awareness.

For Zora Neale Hurston it happened on a boat, in transit, at sea. "I remember the very day that I became colored," she recalled in 1928. She'd been living in her exclusively Black Florida town for all of her thirteen years when she set off for school in Jacksonville. "When I disembarked from the riverboat . . . it seemed that I had suffered a sea change." She became colored in the world, "in my heart as well as in the mirror."

And maybe the slave ship is the threshold of that disembarkment—where the doubled, hyphenated selves got born.

THIS IS WHAT I AM TRYING TO SAY. I AM WRITING TO MAKE EVIdence of my self. I am doing that because, after three decades or so, I have come to realize that the self I thought I had was given to me by somebody else, set upon me a destiny with bad intentions. Becoming a person, forming an identity, had been a sham assignment from the start—for an African American person, there is a multistep process of backtracking and reinterpreting hundreds of years of American history, peeling apart film from adhesive to hold under the light and make out a cloudy reflection.

It's disorienting to be defined by strangers. Before you can actually "become" a psychologically whole human being, before you can "find yourself," you have to first find the fake self and question how it got put there. Then you can burn that fucker up and get on with self-actualizing.

MY CHRISTIAN EDUCATION WAS PURPOSEFULLY UNBALANCED, traditionally incomplete, and uniquely whitewashed. When I first learned about myself, the "African-American," I was made to believe that the origin of my species began here on American soil, tilled by my enslaved ancestors, blah blah blah. I was invented here on this land, already owned, already designated a specific function, assigned a contained and delineated place. I was a fairly recent phenomenon, an advancement of science and global commerce. There were Africans, there were Americans ("Caucasians"?), and then there was me. Hanging on the arm of a mystifying subgroup. "African-American."

Not only did my personal family tree—an elementary school take-home assignment—halt abruptly and unceremoniously, before we had a chance to trace back to queens or warriors, even free Africans or Great Migrationists, but its end, my beginning, was also shrouded and defined by this terrible thing or that: slavery, civil rights—all laced with proper white Christian pity and Clinton-nineties placation. My color was the part of myself even I was implored to ignore and discount. Blackness was taboo: a closed door at the end of a long dark hallway of slaves and black-and-white photos of poodle-skirted protestors. A hall of pain and prejudice, emanating heat. That was then. "I don't see you like that."

Or was it: I don't see you. Or *will not? Cannot unless?*

My skin followed me everywhere; their chanting of "I don't see color" merely a reminder of how I can't escape it. Were it not for my color, I'd be someone who could be seen. But alas. I would have to make do with what I am. Which meant endeavoring to understand every bit of what and who I am, not only as I see it, but as you see it, too; how the television sees it, how your grandpa might see it, how a doctor might see it, other people's mothers, and in the eyes of the law.

Not *make do.* Be spotless.

Not *alas.* Amen.

PROVE THEM WRONG, MY MOM SAID AS I SAT ON HER BED, HELP-ing fold clothes while she watched the nightly news. *This is what they think about us:*

IN *BLACK SKIN, WHITE MASKS,* PSYCHIATRIST FRANTZ FANON wrote that, "The black [person]'s first action is reaction." We have to respond before we get to assert. Not only must we be Black, we "must be black in relation to the white man . . . assessed with regard to [our] degree of assimilation."

As soon as I developed the aptitude to glean from facial and tonal gestures the approximate nature of somebody's prejudgment against me, I set out to devise corrections, like alterations to a dress form. Pavlovian positive reinforcement with every assimilation—which I executed masterfully.

"If I had to define myself," Fanon goes on, "I would say I am in expectation; I am investigating my surroundings; I am interpreting everything on the basis of my findings. I have become a sensor."

Sensing became second nature, the consistent and primary labor of the back of my mind. And were I to miss the abundant dares and degradation embedded into the diction of even my single-digit peers, textbooks, classroom rules, and dress codes, were I not already suspecting that performance and penance would be gravely important to my survival among them if not everyone, their Bible told me so.

We memorized verses weekly. We memorized verses to learn the alphabet. *A: All have sinned and fall short of the glory of God.* We copied down verses to learn penmanship. We were quizzed on biblical figures and their families; we memorized the books of the Old and New Testaments in song; we quoted beatitudes like inside jokes and used Psalms as disses. *B: Believe in the Lord Jesus Christ, and thou shalt be saved.* Homeroom was Bible class. Schoolwide chapel and worship every Wednesday. Senior year Bible focused on preparing us to defend our Christian values in the secular world. *C: Children obey your parents in the Lord, for this is right.* Every morning we pledged two flags with hands over our hearts—the US flag and the Christian flag I'd never seen before and have rarely seen since. They told us we were Christian soldiers, and this was war. *D: Depart from evil, and do good.*

"Onward Christian soldiers," we sang, marching in place

in our Pull-Ups. We were asked, again and again, if we were ready to lay down our lives. To die for our beliefs.

Just as the missionaries in Africa had intended, my early teachings convinced me that the purpose of life was to be good enough to be saved. That you were born into a job, and the job was to prove yourself—through profuse apology and otherworldly self-control—worthy of being born at all. Long before I had time or encouragement to explore my identity, according to me at least, I was concerned with addressing the problem of my soul, an obligation presented as both more urgent and more eternal.

The biggest shame, our biggest shame, is that—as a child doing a simple homework assignment, or on a field trip, receiving hugs in a civil rights exhibit—I so easily internalized my nation's wreckage. That because my sociocultural introduction to myself was framed by sorrow and inadequacy, I felt those things to be both my history and destiny. I internalized the obligation of apologizing, repenting, making up for myself. These were hard tasks to confront, as I did not know what I was apologizing for.

The problem with being the Other is that Other is always worse—abnormal somehow, misfit toys, subpar. Colonialist (or white supremacist) ideology, and its resulting brand of capitalism, depends upon the insinuation that Black lives must matter—*too*. On a human level, culturally and personally, when we think of lives, "Americans," we are not thinking of Black people; otherwise no reminder of our lives mattering would be necessary. When we think "upstanding

American," we do not think of Black people. When we think of Africans, we think of hungry ones. When we think of "African-Americans," we think of slaves.

It's something about that glaring, unsaid, overpronounced hyphen, accentuating and enacting the amendment that advanced us from property to fractional person. That hallowed hyphen, bridging Before and After, redistricting Myth and Fact, as transitive as the slave ship and as stagnant.

The hyphen stands stuck, entropy in either direction, tragically ever in transit between only two ports, trying to make them speak to each other. You could think of it as blank space—the poetic caesura—a backslash, correction, interruption. You could think of it as a body in recline. You could think of it as a boat crossing water.

To start at the beginning: I remember letting a friend lick my arm when she asked if I tasted like chocolate. When somebody got lice, and I had to wait off to the side while each student got their head checked with a little comb, because, I was told, Black people don't get lice. Because of the grease in their hair. The day in middle school a boy asked if I had a gold tooth when my wide-mouthed laugh exposed a filling. At the time, I'd felt poor—someone at the lunch table opens up to model theirs, perfectly camouflaged in pearl coating. Looking back now, I think the boy was looking for my exotic. Expecting it. I'm looking for it, too—what makes me disposable or comical or pitiful. I am looking for something to cling to for solace amid gunfire. I am looking for a root, a pit at the center, something to exorcise and something to embrace.

AT NIGHT

It's probably worth noting that I was an adolescent insomniac, if for no other reason than why, and what I did instead. I worried—worry was both reason and recourse.

That it was sinful to feel, wonder, and want what I did. That the Rapture would come. That angels were watching me. That God could see me digging for gold up my nose. That God could hear me wish my bullies emotional pain. That God knew I was dreading the Rapture. That I was not saved. That I wasn't ready to be judged. That I wouldn't wake up. That I'd wake up to an empty, ruined world. That I was somehow evil or perverted or defective, destined for banishment, and it was only a matter of time before everyone found out—either when I stayed gravitational as they flew into the sky on Jesus's cue, or in some other sinister

way, tomorrow at recess. I worried I was already unforgive-
able.

As I got older, of course, my worries turned to boys and
stuff, grades, what impressions I was making with teachers
or friends, if I shouldn't have said that, why I said that, all
the ways I can and must be better tomorrow. Y2K, and then
anthrax and bin Laden and the general air of "terror" I was
beginning to perceive in every news story, TV show, school
code, sermon, and playground rumor. But there's no way
any of those things is extricable from the rest. By the time
the darkest of such social worries had joined my spiritual
night terrors, I had a TV in my room. Nick at Nite played
until six in the morning, no infomercials.

BY DAY, WHITE TEACHERS MOLDED MY CONSCIENCE AND BE-
havior: how to walk, with a smile and pep; who to pray to
and whose souls to pray for. By day, I was learning to be
vigilant. I was learning what earned adoration and affection,
what might earn me grace. By sleepless, vigilant night, when
I wasn't worrying about my soul, I was absorbing the nostalgia and influences of a baby boomer. By day, "traditional
morals" and impossible standards. By night, "traditional morals," impossible standards.

The development of a Negro child will vary depending
on behaviors modeled, media consumed, lessons absorbed,
and the belief systems to which they are exposed and by
which they are evaluated, such that these beliefs become

the standards by which the child might evaluate themselves. Perhaps their very worth.

In terms of television, I was raised in two timelines. At the turn of the millennium I was consuming mid-century media—Benny Goodman, Louis Armstrong, *I Love Lucy*, *Bewitched*—alongside *TRL*, Sugar Ray, and Christina Aguilera's "Genie in a Bottle" video.

By day, it was the 1950s in class and the '90s at lunchtime, and by night, on the cusp of sleep, it was the interiors of 1960s family homes and 1970s offices, a desert island with white Urkel and a big-titted blonde, a flirty blond genie whose very wink was a spell. I remain one of the only millennials familiar with *Rhoda*. All of it twirled and twisted in my young head.

By night, even in drowsy anguish, I soaked in Brady family ideals and Mary Tyler Moore idolatry, the "values" that reared my teachers, and I absorbed it with the knowledge that their vision and version of the truth was the one that mattered most in terms of my salvation. In terms of what was the right way to be.

This is all to say, maybe, that I am used to sorting and sifting through information and making my own sense of it, and that I have an unusually long, historical view of the politics of desirability, entertainment, and aspiration.

OVER THE LATE '90S AND EARLY 2000S, I BEGAN TO USE NICK AT Nite programming as a measure of time and anxiety. If

Happy Days was on, I wasn't too worried, there was still time for a solid night's sleep. *Taxi* was cause for mild panic: a good night's sleep no longer possible. *Newhart*, followed by *The Bob Newhart Show*, meant time for reckoning. It was creeping up on five thirty, and my only hope was to power nap through the sales pitches for frying pans and Medicaid.

Certain shows I skipped, and either fell asleep or buzzed the TV back on when they were over. Andy Griffith whistle, instant mute, and roll over—it's still early, not even midnight. *All in the Family* or *Sanford and Son*, too brash. *Happy Days*, often just way too happy, from the second the coin hits the jukebox. I usually turned off *The Beverly Hillbillies* after mouthing along to the theme song. Sometimes, I turned off the TV after Mary Tyler Moore tossed her hat with a little spin, not sure why. She was clever, sharp. Not a kitchen-bound housewife or a sex genie, not swooning over "*swimming pools, movie stars.*" She was good at her job, Rhoda was awesome, and I'd still wear every single one of their outfits.

I was familiar with Mary from *The Dick Van Dyke Show*, which Nick at Nite had been running for a while before airing *The Mary Tyler Moore Show*, which I gleaned after one or two viewings was not related. While I missed the L-shaped couch and mid-century tables of the Van Dyke household that would no doubt inform my future design tastes, Independent Mary was an upgrade. She was girl power.

Everybody wanted to root for her, the show was about rooting for her, and, subconsciously, her exhilarated grin picked at my self-esteem. As a young girl with big-city ambitions and my own "spunk," I understood that Mary was meant to reassure and inspire us. But something about the easy way she flings her hat into the air—how just by arriving, she's already made it—told me my success was not as certain. Nice to know it was possible for someone, I guess. My best friend at the time, smiley and theatrical, bore some resemblance.

How can Mary just do that? I remember thinking in the dark. All those people rushing in the busy square, and her arms stretched wide as she twirls, oblivious, without consequences.

ARE
WE NOT
ENTERTAINERS?

My cab driver to the courthouse on this June morning, Roy, asks if I can give him "a little shine" by mentioning him here. Roy is a big fan of Bill Cosby.

"Do you think he did it?" Roy asks, and I say I don't know. We're late, I'm tired, I don't feel like having the same conversation over and over.

The night before, heading back from the Montgomery County Courthouse in Norristown, Pennsylvania, to my hotel one town over, my cab driver announced, "The only thing is, why did they wait until now?" I was too tired to answer then, but at this point, with Roy, we're yoked. I'm invested. We're in this thing—the fifteen-minute drive— together. Roy has the same suspicions as last night's driver, and most radio and talk show commentators, too.

"Man, they wait until Bill gets all old and then start saying all this shit about him. My thing is, why did they wait so long? Why is it coming out now?"

"Because."

"Because the powers that be didn't want it to come out."

"Well, maybe. But also, who would believe those women? We barely believe them now, right, so who would have believed them then?"

"All these women talking about he gave them a pill . . . Bill, man, it's too many people saying you did it."

"That's what I'm saying."

"I should say he gave me a pill, get some of that money. 'Well, he put a pill in my Jell-O pudding and next thing I know I was fast asleep.'"

It takes me a minute to realize Roy is trying to make me laugh. Roy laughs.

"I don't think it's that simple. It seems pretty tough to make a case, actually."

In the case of the *Commonwealth v. William Henry Cosby, Jr.*, for the sexual assault of Andrea Constand, the defense motioned that Ms. Constand and any other complainants not be referred to as "victims."

Before I even get to the trial, I am feeling horrible about being a woman, as usual. How I must see myself through the eyes of men, anxious about the preferred way to look and be. How I see myself in contrast with white women, a holdover instinct from my suburban upbringing, reinforced by television. I am not preferred. I will do in a pinch. Good enough. Emily and Amanda and Rachel are preferred, their mild opinions and floral skirts, their lilting giggles, the way they tuck oak-brown hair behind their ears.

Very early, I learned that selecting and nailing a role was crucial to social and emotional survival, that there was always an audience. If I could just do and say the right thing in the right way for the right people . . . It's how I ended up turning to writing, when my face and body betrayed me, wouldn't act right.

Recess was my training camp. Among my many performance-based recess activities—including multiple *My So-Called Life*–inspired television shows with rehearsed opening song montages, set on the monkey bars when we could get to them—was house. Playing house, people sort of fall into their assumed, assigned, or ancestral roles. The most white girl of all the white girls always called dibs on being the teenage daughter—the best character, we knew, the most desirable on any TV show. Most frequently, this character was a hybrid beast: part Cher Horowitz, part Kelly Kapowski, part Kelly Bundy. Another kind of white girl would announce herself as mother and very quickly assign the planned-all-along husband; a hyper kid who doesn't really want to be there becomes an uncontrollable baby; the girls French braiding each other's hair call themselves twins.

Usually the assembling household suggested two options for my role: the adopted daughter or the family dog. In either case, the presence of my color needed to be explained. I was an extension, something hanging off a branch of the tree in the backyard of the very "house" itself.

This is how I learned to entertain.

My role as token was (and is) complex—a psychological performance dependent on flexibility and charm. Among my friends, I was the appointed informant of Black life, charged with the responsibility to dispel its mystery, disprove its stereotypes, and represent its exceptionalism. That's how I learned about acceptance—and its price.

Seated near me in the overflow courtroom designated for the press, a trio of white women reporters (seersucker, wedding rings, ballet flats) are making small talk, reminiscing about covering the Dylann Roof trial. So horrible, in contrast with how truly good the victims were. So forgiving, exceptional people. They weren't asking for it.

They are the same girls who'd posed next to me in blue-and-white school T-shirts, easily comfortable in their skorts. Every bland thing about them sparkled. When I met them again in college, I could see their futures. Wedding planning over cocktails on the Upper East Side in head-to-toe J.Crew, or sipping iced coffees in Lululemon, while I'm on a barstool reading poetry, getting older. I'm not the same as them. There are different rules for me.

I wonder if, even after all these lessons on being—at least appearing—exceptional, I would be somebody who was asking for it. The character next to your name is the part you get, and you take it and add red bottoms and a graduate degree, maybe a plate of oysters or whatever. You'll still be a woman, you'll still be a certain kind of woman, and men will always see what they want.

When it comes to violence against women, it doesn't matter who goes to the Hamptons, whose hair is thin and gold, who gets to be a feminist, who inherits the bank. Misogyny and bigotry breed a common indiscriminate urge. They both hurt, in uniquely discriminate ways. I'm one of maybe three Black women in the room, which means I'm one of three women wrestling with that familiar triple-consciousness chicken or egg. Am I Black today or a woman? Where do I pledge allegiance? Which injustices should I fight first?

Before the trial even began, I texted a friend: "Can't we burn the men and keep the culture?" In support of and solidarity with his victims (however Mr. Cosby's defense attorneys insist they be labeled), many folks had been quick to disavow Cosby, his influence, and his body of work—all of it tarnished by his crimes. Spoiled pudding.

After learning, from his own autobiography, that Miles Davis "slapped the shit out of" his then-wife Cicely Tyson, Pearl Cleage wrote in refrain: "He is guilty of self-confessed violent crimes against women such that we should break his albums, burn his tapes and scratch his CDs until he acknowledges and apologizes and agrees to rethink his position on The Woman Question." The great Miles Davis had scored entire phases of the writer's life, kept her company and kept her inspired, but "either we think it's a crime to hit us or we don't."

"Can we keep giving our money to Miles Davis so that he can buy a Malibu beach house and terrorize our sisters in it?" she asks. "Can we continue to celebrate the genius in the face of the monster?"

Why should Bill Cosby be rewarded with any more attention, loyalty, or money? Many of us were conflicted. How could we just act as if *A Different World* hadn't influenced our college aspirations, as if *The Cosby Show* hadn't served as a key piece of evidence proving our humanity to the early nineties masses? Can't we burn the man and keep the culture?

It's impossible to discuss the rise and glory of Black comedy within a newly integrated America without including Bill Cosby's legacy on the stage and screen. And it's hard to talk about the "color-blind" ideology and respectability politics of the nineties—the kind that raised me to defer to and mimic Amanda in her floral skirt—without invoking *The Cosby Show* as the vision board for Wholesome Blacks. Forget the Jeffersons' wide-eyed "movin' on up," these Negroes were up, man. Sky-high and sitting comfortably, almost unrecognizable in their ease and achievement.

For most of us, and certainly for my working-class family, the Cosbys weren't representation, they were inspiration. A doctor and a lawyer? Very Special Episodes? It wasn't even subtle. We could be funny without being broke or salacious. We could be a family unit tighter than the Brady Bunch. We could go to college, hang out with Stevie Wonder, learn valuable lessons, be Black without being *that* Black. Unabashedly aspirational.

In 1987, my parents sat up in their waterbed watching an episode of *The Cosby Show*, my dad afro'd and my mom's stomach swelling with would-be me. Morgan was a bit part, some little friend of Rudy's with a precocious attitude. That's where I come from: aspirational, family-values, American Dream Black.

Absent any threat, any Scary Black Man associations, Cosby heralded a particular type of post-revolution Respectable Black Man that illustrated a cultural obsession with capital—and assimilation—that presided over 1980s America. Bill Cosby's classification as a Black Man was incidental. In the white imagination, the must-see-TV landscape, he was *I'm not Black, I'm O. J.* assimilated. Funny, but never too political, never disruptive. Well-behaved.

Unlike acerbic Black comics like Richard Pryor and Dick Gregory, Cosby's mainstream success wasn't rooted in what he said or did—it was how he said it, what skin he had on while doing it. His radicalism—and his weapon—was his wholesomeness. Whereas Gregory marched for civil rights, and Pryor turned the angry, sexualized Black man stereotype on its head, Cosby's shock value was ultimately in his success: as a father, a career man, a chaser of American morality. Brushed up as it was against the increasing consequences of upward mobility within the Black community, Cosby's popularity was an antidote to the absent, neglectful, drug-addled Black man white media relied upon. It was important just to see him sitting in that living room, answering the door to that brownstone.

In the third-season episode that fortuitously inspired my naming, young Morgan reveals she's allergic to olives, having already eaten some—but, she chirps, she feels good so far! [Audience laughter.] I come from this, too: self-destructive impulses, swallowing what I shouldn't, becoming a punchline. If they are laughing, they aren't afraid, and I am safe because I'm safe to them.

Sometimes I wonder if our persistence, the very audacity of our continuance, is part of the joke.

THE PROSECUTION HAS RESTED, AND THE DEFENSE CALLS ONE witness (it isn't Cosby, it's the arresting officer, who's already provided a statement on behalf of the prosecution) for a six-minute testimony before their closing statement, delivered by a middle-aged folksy-type white man with a slight New Jersey accent and a screeching fervency. Before this morning's proceedings, I'd watched him hyperactively rock back and forth in his chair, flit around the courtroom chatting and laughing with the other attorneys, drum casually on the table. This man would come to be My Enemy, and I shall refer to him, henceforth, as such.

It's noticeable in this world who takes up space and who is comfortable.

On the carpet of the family room in our small house in Southern California, my early TV memories are correlated with my nascent understanding of morality and decorum. How to be Good. Regularly scheduled episodes of *The Fresh Prince of Bel-Air* were interrupted by coverage of the O. J. Simpson chase. Regularly scheduled episodes of *The Cosby Show* were preceded by news segments about Rodney King.

In *The Cosby Show* nineties, everyone was saying, "I don't see color." Willful ignorance was in style; we called it progress. On the playground of my white private school, I worked hard to prove myself an exception, a pleasant surprise to the usual narrative. With a little help from the Huxtables, I learned how to be Respectable in spite of my skin. *You're not Black, you're just Morgan.*

Now, as the trial judge asks Cosby a series of questions to confirm that he has not been persuaded or coerced by his counsel or anyone else, the Comedian is performing. He is reminding everyone in the room who he is, that he's been in their homes, made them laugh, always made them feel safe. The Great Assimilator, the Great Unifier, the Jell-O guy. It's familiar behavior: deception, charm.

My Enemy is an actor, too. He embarks on a monologue about a recent visit to Shake Shack wherein he was stricken with nostalgia upon the sight of a father and daughter. This little tale has nothing to do with anything—it's a spell, the way his voice rises and falls, the way he uses his hands in descriptions, peppers the speech with self-deprecating jokes. He gazes at the jury and it is a plea. Be on my side, he's purring, it's the only logical side. He talks about how the father spoon-fed a milkshake to his three-year-old daughter. "After each spoonful," he recalls, "he would give her a kiss. I miss those days! She looked at him like she was looking at God!"

That's when a guffaw escapes me into the baited quiet of the courtroom. I put my hand over my mouth, rolling my eyes, and other reporters turn and frown at me sternly. But, come on! I can't believe the theater. My Enemy talks about how when children grow up, they see that their parents are imperfect, that "the only angels are in heaven."

"Mr. Cosby taught us how to smile," he says. "He taught us how to love each other, no matter what we look like, no matter how different we are."

Bingo. Shameless sweet-talking, manipulation. That's what the justice system is: a talent show. He's good. For good measure, before diving into the facts of the case, My Enemy gives the jury a quick-and-dirty definition of words like *burden* and *reasonable doubt*. He reminds them that the United States has the highest burden of proof of anywhere in the world. He says, "We defend innocence at all costs."

Cosby is no angel, is maybe what he's saying, we should know that by now. When children grow up, they see that people just can't help themselves.

"THIS IS THE SAME COURT I WAS IN," ROY TELLS ME. "FOR CUS-tody of my son. If I never spend another minute inside a courtroom I will be a happy man. Spent so many hours in there arguing with that woman. But I won, I'm happy, my son's happy. She's not happy, though. But what are you gonna do."

"Oh. Yeah, I don't know."

I have been trying to figure Roy out. There are Black men who align themselves with Black men, and there are Black men who align themselves with Black people. Would I have a beer with Roy? I wonder. How long before he calls a woman a liar?

A lot of Black people, Roy-types and other types, clung tightly to Cosby's presumed innocence even as allegations and evidence piled up. They would remain big fans of Bill Cosby, even if they thought he was guilty. Like several men before him, he would be excused. What are you gonna do?

While I personally can't say that Bill Cosby taught me how to love my fellow human beings, his irreversible influence made accepting his guilt complicated for a lot of us, even if our problem wasn't believing the women, or simply squaring fandom with condemnation of the artist's behavior.

In the case of the *Common Black Woman v. William Henry Cosby Jr.*, I see no innocence to defend; Cosby's fall from purity was his own doing. But can't we burn the man and keep what's ours? Maybe we are clinging to the parts of ourselves that owed so much to what the Cosbys represented, the pride we'd felt watching them. Can't we keep our comfort?

IN THE COURTROOM, COSBY'S ORIGINAL TESTIMONY TO THE POlice is read aloud, line by line. I feel gobsmacked—violated—by the way intimacy is described and defined. How romance is defined, how touch is regarded as conversation.

I'm rubbing the middle, which is the skin, just about the trousers . . . I'm giving Andrea time to say yes or no about an area that is right there in the question zone.

I didn't say it verbally. The action is in my hand on her midriff, which is skin . . . I don't hear her say anything.

Somewhere between permission and rejection. I am not stopped.

Words and actions can be misinterpreted and unless you are a supreme being, you cannot know how someone else will interpret it.

I tell her to go to sleep . . . I make tea for her. Red Zinger. She said she's had it before . . . I wanted her to relax and go to sleep after we had our necking session.

The jury asks for a definition of "without her permission." I would like a definition of "the question zone."

Taking seriously his job to "defend innocence at all costs," My Enemy proceeds to engage in a thought exercise designed to eviscerate the victim's behavior and its rationality. Its "truth."

"You'd never forget to tell the police that you went to dinner if you were sexually assaulted. You'd never forget the details of that night."

My Enemy is anyone who can so easily diminish another person's pain, who is able to dismiss the effects of trauma as imagined or misremembered, who refuses to be sensitive to the pain of another person—even a woman. I'm jealous of his privilege to be able to freely make such broad claims and assumptions, to garner nods from jurors. Assumptions are why we are at this trial.

He continues to fix his mouth to use the word *romantic*. He continues to revise the story Andrea reported.

"If my wife and I were sitting by a fire drinking brandy, she would call it romantic. So why would Andrea say that Mr. Cosby wasn't being affectionate? Why?!? I don't understand it!"

He's raising his voice, passionately frustrated, and I perceive a kind of hatred, a disgust. He resents when women disturb, when they don't do what they're supposed to.

My Enemy has never been a woman.

My Enemy, perhaps, has never even listened to a woman's

account of living in the world. It's worse that the male reporters in our room are chuckling at the callous way he makes fun of the victim, and worse still that the women are. The worst part is the way he's shouting, spewing acidity, speaking on behalf of what all Reasonable People must think about women—why would you find yourself in a room again with a man who assaulted you? Why would you contact him, if it made you so uncomfortable? Why would you talk on the phone to a girlfriend for forty-five minutes after seeing Mr. Cosby if you aren't gossiping about your relationship? ("If I stayed on the phone for forty-five minutes with my wife, she'd think I was having an affair" is the More Reasonable Logic My Enemy offers in contrast. At no point in the proceedings does his wife take the stand to corroborate his supposition.) "Why not call it a relationship?"

All I can think, all I can mutter under my breath, feeling my forehead and cheeks get hot, is *Because*. Because, dude. Because because because of this. Because of everything.

"When you left Pittsburgh," My Enemy says to the members of the jury, who have been imported to avoid a tainted jury pool of publicity-swayed locals, "you didn't leave your common sense. Stop This!!!"

The drama, the accent, the shouting, the attempt to charm, to buddy up, to appeal to a particularly privileged logic. I don't need to hear much more. Or, I've already heard it, learned it. The words press on me, I feel them wriggling around in my brain, trying to change my mind. My conclusion, slipping out of the courtroom shaking my head and sucking my teeth before My Enemy's monologue reaches its big finish: Men know everything. They know what they would do, which is what anyone, any logical respectable person would do. They know what women are thinking, what women say to one another, how women will react before they do. They know how narrative works. They know how to perform. Are we not entertained?

One thing I love about comedy is the permission to act up, to step out of the Respectable and Well-Behaved skin without consequence. Comedy is perpetual forgiveness.

That was inappropriate, but it was funny, so I forgive you. I know you were just joking. You didn't mean it like that. You got carried away. You didn't hear me say no. You forgot to ask for my consent. You're right—I'm overreacting. You're right—maybe it didn't happen the way I remember. I forgive you. I'm sorry. Will you forgive me?

FROM THE BACK SEAT I WATCH ROY SHAKE HIS HEAD THE WAY all Black men do. He knows someone is pulling the strings, controlling the narrative, and he's halfway right.

"I believe in all that stuff, you know, conspiracies, Illuminati. It's out there. They made Michael Jordan go play baseball because his image was tarnished by gambling with gangsters. It was the powers that be that made him. I feel a little sorry for Bill."

"I feel sorry for the women," I mumble, craning my head from the back seat to make sure he hasn't taken another wrong turn.

"I just don't understand. You got all that money. You got

women who want to sleep with you! Why do you resort to that?"

"I don't think it's really about that." I tuck away his use of the word *resort* to contend with at a much later date. There are too many levels of complexity to process at once.

"You think it's like . . . a sickness?"

"Power."

"Right. That's a sickness. Is Bill pulling up right now? You think I can get a picture?"

BLACK PEOPLE DON'T GO TO THERAPY

My first therapist was a middle-aged white woman, and as such, I could only imagine her to be conservative, Christian, and cut off from any other kinds of lives that might exist. I could only imagine she was exactly like all the middle-aged white women that populated my life at school and in our suburb, by whom I consistently felt judged. I struggled to understand the political terms of our relationship. All of which I might have discovered through talk therapy, had my therapist not been a middle-aged white woman. I didn't know how safe I was. How much of myself I was safe to be.

I also just didn't know what to do, how the whole thing worked. My only exposure to "therapy" was from books set in New England about wealthy white ladies, Woody Allen talking about his "analyst," the insult "you need therapy," and *Frasier*. Antidepressants were "crazy pills," a lifelong sentence to social alienation.

"Black people don't go to therapy," my dad had said when I begged my parents to call me a psychiatrist. I was fifteen and I didn't want to die, exactly, but living had suddenly become excruciating, each day the same or worse than the one before, and that summer, a few pages into *Prozac Nation*, no pages into the summer reading I usually whizzed through before July, I knew that either I couldn't feel like this or didn't have to. Therapy was my second-to-last resort, the only other option, I cried while clutching a kitchen knife.

Summer has always been my season since then. Gloom descends with winter like it does for everyone, but there's something about tank tops making their debuts and sweat beads crawling down my neck that lures the very worst of my depression. Something about the weight of the air, relentless sun bleeding through ozone, sets an idea in the recessed hallways of my mind. It's the idea of my death.

Symptoms of depression I exhibited in childhood had gone undetected or labeled me a spoiled brat. Panic attacks read as tantrums. Mood swings were me being fifteen. I had always been emotional, sensitive. (People usually spoke those words with frustration or disdain.) This was not just my angst and bad attitude, I knew. It couldn't be. This wasn't normal pain—this wasn't livable.

I was told to be strong, that my people had always been strong, that their strength was mine, too. But when I looked with dread into my future, on days when I could bear to imagine one, I wondered, *How strong?* How strong do you need to be to want to die—and yet keep living? "How much is a nigger supposed to take?" Toni Morrison wrote in *Beloved*.

Knowing where to start—even admitting the need for therapy, considering it an option—left an unknown frontier before my family. In our small conservative suburb, there was no model for a Black teenager seeing a psychologist—and that I was breaking a generational cultural norm was not lost on me. If Blackness was essentially defined by resilience through unimaginable struggle, what indeed did I really have to cry about?

I learned to point back to myself as the problem. I prayed harder. Chastised myself with more frequency and fervency. Black people don't do therapy. Slaves didn't need therapy. What was so special, so wrong, about me?

It occurs to me only now that this cultural taboo is likely why I hadn't always talked about race in therapy, or why I hadn't acknowledged its intrinsic connection to my mental health. How could I, when tons of Black people were walking around seeming fine, when my disorders were a product of my brain malfunction, and mine alone to bear? Back then, I thought going to therapy was the least Black thing about me—and I listened to indie rock.

While puzzling frantically over how to best perch myself on my high school therapist's couch and second-guessing my choice to wear a *secular* band tee, worried she was somehow in cahoots with my Bible teacher, it had never occurred to me that I could say anything negative about white people there, or say "white people" at all. Talking about Blackness with this lady was not the road to becoming a normal teenager, to "getting better." I just wanted to be invited to movie night.

My primary goal for beginning therapy had been to effectively extirpate from my mind any suicidal thoughts and impulses, stamp out all my wrong things. My difference had always been clear to me and those around me, but it had been easy enough to craft into a "quirky" personality, lean on my sociability, become hilarious, and cling to writing—the thing that felt most naturally me.

People are allowed to be strange. You don't recover from "crazy." *Disabled* wasn't just a label, it was an unshakable identity. I already had so many of those.

My thoughts weren't so much something to be examined as something to abolish, cast out. That's why I hid them there, in word choice and sentence structure. Becoming a writer had been paramount to my survival method for multiple reasons. Mostly, to contextualize my aesthetic tastes (e.g., blazers) and bookish, indoor nature, and to disguise my developing social phobia and signs of depression. Writing has never been my therapy, because writing is not therapy. Therapy is therapy.

While over the years I've gotten better at detecting oncoming depressive episodes, sometimes it's only reading my work back that makes me realize I'm depressed. Writing has been an important way for me to see myself, and socially, claiming the label "writer" made me make sense. And in that way, I realize now, I thought it made up for me. Because I was convinced I needed making up for.

If you see yourself as something to be corrected rather than someone to be helped, it's easy not to realize that help is even an option. Many of us don't even bother asking. It took a while for me to approach therapy as more than a self-initiated challenge to fix my social aberrations, a sort of pain management specialist I need to frequent in order to monitor my depression, and it took years for me to recognize its potential for radical self-understanding and sociocultural awareness. It took me even longer to bring up the slave ship in a session, and even longer than that to get a Black therapist.

I have grown up with therapy and my conception of therapy has grown up with me. I've grown to love sharing the burden of what I once called self-hatred but I now know was something else, something embedded before birth. I've grown to appreciate and rely on the way therapy and psychiatry can help you understand how you see, maybe even why, wherein the why is, among other things, white supremacy and specifically the kind begat in slavery. This is yet another example of white supremacy's double conundrum, its two-sided knife: how all the reasons Black people don't go to therapy—its reliance upon a culturally discriminatory, if not invalidating, norm; its potential for devious social control; its societal stigma; its out-of-reach expense; the reminder that slaves didn't need therapy ("and look what they survived!")—all that is because of white supremacy, which also happens to be the reason Black people need and deserve quality therapy. You can't live with it, but you're not allowed to live without it sticking to the walls of your brain like vines. It keeps you awake, dark summer night after sweaty night, thinking *How dare you hope for what you'll never have.*

EVERYTHING
IS A
SLAVE SHIP

For example, reading poems about dead Black people to an all-white crowd in August 2014, after the police gunned down three in one week, on a wood plank stage in a makeshift basement bar, I am also in the belly of a slave ship, claustrophobic and wondering which one of us is next. In an unfamiliar bed underneath a white man, I'm on a slave ship. Paying taxes, there I am, on the boat, wondering how I got there. The slave ship could be a football field, a house party, a happy meal. I have a visual memory and an emotional one. I see reminders of the boat as sure and as frequently as I feel its symptoms and residue.

Professor Christina Sharpe calls it "the wake"—the slave ship's wreckage, the boat's murky remnants. How we remember, and how our bodies do. In her book *Lose Your*

Mother, Saidiya Hartman calls it "the afterlife of slavery"—how we are stuck, how we are haunted, and how our bodies haunt this land.

Every day, another funeral, another wake. The specific ache that started on the boat and never let the stench of death rub off. The way we mourn and celebrate in one breath. The way we are always back then, even now.

"Living in the wake means living the history and present of terror," writes Sharpe, "as the ground of our everyday Black existence," adding that in a lot of public discourse, "we, Black people, become *carriers* of terror."

We are in the wake, and we are the wake.

As in the wake of a ship. As in the wake we attend daily. As in the awakeness of African American awareness. As in the wake of disaster. As in "rituals through which we enact grief and memory." And, "in the wake, the semiotics of the slave ship continue."

What we know, imprecisely, about the boat on the ocean is that there are spirits there. Imagine an oasis off the radar of linear planes, suspended as bodies in transit from unwelcome shore to unwelcome shore, deck to death by drowning. In *The Long Emancipation*, Rinaldo Walcott writes, "If, in another moment, Black cargoes confined to holds of ships could simultaneously be a liability and a profit, that time is with us still." The slave ship, standing still.

"Ships that traverse the seas like cruise ships and fishing boats now bear an indelible link to each other through the logics of slavery," he points out. "The ship remains a force in the lives of Black peoples. The ship remains a signifier of global white supremacy, uneven wealth and Black enslave-ment, African colonization, and a set of global logics that continually place Black life-forms outside of the category of the human."

Ours, he writes, is an unfinished process of emancipa-tion. In our fight to get free, we're backtracking not only in search of our origin, but also in order to undo ourselves as merchandise, as a thing used to support a larger, dubious system. Because the origin is economic. Our cultural con-sciousness is filled with signifiers of the economics of the boat.

Think of the slave ship as a yacht, the inherent violence of leisure. A cruise ship, where you almost forget you're pay-ing to be there. A commercial cargo ship, shuttling to sell.

We are in the money. We were the start-up cash. The slave ship is the dollar bill framed above the register: the first profits.

Walcott contends that the "ghost" of the slave ship "is both an event and a first time, but, importantly, it is also repetition."

It teems with energy—the ramifications perpetuating and reverberating into the future and what Americans call the past—where our souls go and a story of us begins, the wrong to be corrected, the tightly tangled root ball of insta-bility, uncertainty; why I feel unsafe, or call myself inade-quate, or don't ask for what I need; the particular anxiety, the sunken panic of realizing: You are at sea.

The slave ship is: the hyphen, the water, *the wake*, the boat, the origin, the unbecoming, the American economy, the myth, the moment, both end and beginning (as death always is), a site and a situation, a rupture, a transformation, a template. Because when it is not a slave ship it's a plantation, which is to say there is always the cage of not an identity but a story of one. When I say this is violent I mean ownership always is. When I say plantation I mean the continued and echoed circumstance of ownership and entrapment. I have a physical memory, a sensory one. There is a memory of my body taking up space on this land. The memory of my unallowed personality. Identifiable, with no identity.

The slave ship has become a place of mind. It's where we are held hostage from self-definition, where freedom of self is an aberration to the order of things. The order that is embedded in you and in the Western tradition, which you and we in ways large and despicable and slight, uphold and worship even when it serves none of us—merely because we have not had a look at where these wrongs may have begun and why they might still reign over us.

Maybe our story began when the dimensions of the boat were crafted, when the cells below decks were sketched. Maybe it started the moment the deal was made among trader and purchaser. Was it upon capture, or pending completion of the transatlantic journey, conditional upon surviving the conditions of the boat? Was it the new names—purely for inventory? Was it the auction block? Was it the shackle? The Christian baptism under White Jesus's watch?

I arrive back at the slave ship by process of elimination, exhaustion, and experiment, having exhausted alternate beginnings. We never shared shores, languages, goddesses—but everybody was on the boat. I arrive at the boat by listening to how our stories leave their mouths and which ones were left out. I arrive seeking origins of a particularly sinister definition of us, specifically how much we're worth.

It is imprecise. But it is a certain, recognizable port, a point of reference and therefore, maybe, reverence. Certain as the water, specifically the Atlantic, all the way under it—and also the sky, witnessing, receiving our home-goers rising from underwater, the souls thrown aboard—I imagine them above us and below us, even now. That's the boat. A passage through.

If you think about the boat as a moment of birth, origin or rupture, catalyst of hyphenation, it's death, too. Leaving one world for another, if we believe there are other worlds, which we must. The ship is a time of death, the stamped ending. Irreversible destruction of an "identity" which is just to say humanness—Africanness or citizenness. Loss of a kind of certainty and safety that no human should be able to dictate for another.

And if you think of the boat as an imprecise location in approximately the middle of the Atlantic ocean as the Black American big bang, starting with the removal of the person, the rebranding as goods, then slaves then fugitives then cooks then soldiers then coons then hyphenated citizens then diversity then back to goods then Hulk-like monsters to be put down then Black lives then presidents and back to dead Black usta-coulda been a life. Usta-coulda been sane, been gentle. Not no more. Not by now.

The boat could function like a graveyard, a mausoleum, representing both heaven and hell, which is to say any imagined afterlife that is still a life. A catacomb of possibility and torture. The echoing haunting deep down: Am I even a person?

I arrive at the boat finding no other roots. Nothing else behind me. Behind the trees. Behind what I know for certain was lost. The boat is the more to the story. The function of a bridge where on either side, nobody knows what to do with you. The mode in which I got here: not from, or where to, but how—through whose means, in whose chains. Only thing that's for sure is the how, which is to say in transit, unsettled, unarrived. Which is to say I never arrived, "came," but maybe that's what they think, why they think and shoot like they do.

To propagate and grow a vining houseplant, make leaf cuttings with an inch or two of stem on either side. Place the stems of each leaf in water, making sure the leaf nodes are completely submerged. As roots grow from each node, they will begin to entangle, creating a root system. A single root is good for nothing; a stemmed leaf is dead without a node.

I only know the how. I can only strive to reclaim and correct the *how*ness of our origin; to either leap off the boat, or Amistad that sucker.

The boat is rupture and eruption. Which is not erasure. The boat proves erasure is not possible, only submergence, perversion. The rupture is psychological and metaphysical and threefold: spiritual, social, subconscious.

A rupture. A tear. It was never meant to be gentle.

WE
GOT
JOKES

Richard Pryor said all Black humor started on slave ships. The joke, from his album *Bicentennial Nigger*, goes: "Cat was on his way over here, rowin', and another dude said, *'Whatchoo laughin about?'* He said, 'Yesterday I was a king.'"

It's funny when Black people be saying that we're descendants of royalty, all of us kings and queens, but we know it isn't true, and it's even sadder and funnier that nobody can actually prove otherwise. Might as well say what you want. Might as well make "fact" a white lie, this being the first, the one they told us about ourselves. Who's to say? You have to laugh. The way we remind ourselves to soothe ourselves, rewrite ourselves, re-own ourselves.

King stands for everything we could have been—all the kingdoms we would have reigned.

Let the slave ship stand for the beginning: of language, comedy, soul, religion, culture, and class. Let the slave ship symbolize the oceans it crosses, the deep where bodies lie and the open sky where souls rise. Let it mean those lost and those unborn. Our history and our future, both blurry with seafoam and selective cultural memory.

Let it stand for grief and let it stand for *king*. Let it be a joke and let it stand for threat. A place, a thing, a People.

Let yesterday stand for unknown. Let the whole thing stand for the nakedness of living and dying without a beginning, let the whole thing stand for everything lost in the water.

Maybe Black Americans have already reclaimed the trajectory of the boat—innovators of drumbeats and bards of selfhood, preacher-poets, bodies shining in the sun all glamour and lust, frighteningly innovative, writing even as we row.

GEORGE BUSH DOESN'T CARE ABOUT BLACK PEOPLE

e watched the YouTube clip over and over in the high school library during a research period for my AP American Government class: Kanye West standing next to Mike Myers on a Hurricane Katrina telethon, the hilarious looks on both their faces when he blurts, "George Bush doesn't care about Black people." Even my Ronald Reagan–obsessed teacher—the one who threw up his hands in relief when I walked in late one day after an orthodontist appointment because, in my absence, he apparently could not bring himself to discuss the liberal half of things—giggled as he indulged us in another and another viewing, like spoonfuls of chocolate sprinkles on Pinkberry.

I remember wondering why I was laughing, and if we were all laughing at the same thing. And it wasn't Kanye

West we couldn't get enough of—though we (my white classmates, plus me) were properly conditioned to translate an unpredictable and flashy Black rapper as the equivalent of a cartoon banana peel—it was Mike Myers's flummoxed reaction, how his whole world seemed to drop out of his body with his stomach.

I could watch Aghast Mike Myers all day. It's like watching a live birth—the moment teeming with infinite possibility. As a group, of course, my white conservative class had winced with sympathy for the Austin Powers guy. Stripped of fake teeth and a fake accent, and incongruously paired with a Grammy-winning rapper, he seemed especially normal, even proper. He embodied thoughts and prayers. This also appeared to be the held view of the producers and most other guests of the telethon—a knee-jerk pathologizing of Black anger.

If I were teaching the clip in a creative writing class, I would laud its clean narrative structure. In mere minutes, the viewer can identify the hero and the villain, the realms of status quo and interruption, sane versus insane. The collective gasp comes when Kanye's speech veers emotional— What is he talking about? Why is he "ranting"? Who is this angry, inarticulate person?—and the belly laugh comes when Myers's gaze juts sideways like a shiver, when he redirects the moment, glossy-eyed with bewilderment, and restores teleprompted order. Nice save. Kanye West, the walking post–9/11 bomb threat. Kanye West, predecessor to the shoe chucked at George Bush's head during a press conference three years later. Kanye West, disturber of peace. I could watch Kanye West say "George Bush doesn't care about Black people" all day. It's just so funny.

I'm not a comedian or anything, but I'm a fairly hilarious person, one who thinks quite a bit about how words work. I know we laugh when we're uncomfortable, and we cry when we laugh; those urges sit in our chests, two-headed. I know the best jokes hurt, that they needle at you slowly because they are rooted in the most unspeakable truths. I love real shit and sad jokes.

I often use humor to talk about my darkest aches and the country's most egregious defects, and it is always so satiating. Maybe a joke's success depends on its particular understanding of pain.

In *Laughing Fit to Kill*, Glenda Carpio writes that "Black American humor began as a wrested freedom." Laughing at and in the midst of slavery's injustices, and "despite the life-threatening injunctions against black laughter," was a profound form of "affirming their humanity in the face of its violent denial." Our humor has always been multipurpose. In protest, in praise, in order to shade, shame, or blame—to claim and reclaim our agency. How could slavery, she asks, become a subject of humor? Only in such a tragicomedy of this boat, where "laughter is dissociated from gaiety and is, instead, a form of mourning."

Ismail Muhammad noted in the *Los Angeles Review of Books* how Kanye's telethon moment predates the artist's "crafted" public image as an irreverent, outrageous, and even poignant antagonist. The Kanye West of today has a slew of public outbursts on record, from a thirteen-minute speech and presidential bid in 2015 to infamously interrupting Taylor Swift's acceptance speech at the 2009 MTV Video Music Awards. But "George Bush doesn't care about Black people" is a markedly different statement than "Beyoncé had one of the best videos of all time."

It was improvised, not stylized—its urgency and potency is in its awkwardness. "Kanye's mournful and broken speech," Muhammad recalls, "erodes the telethon's universalism, provides a window into black America's emotional life." The shock of Kanye's leap off-script reverberated beyond the cameras.

It's funny—and it's scary—because it's uncomfortable. Because it's a moment of trespass and rupture. It was the stilted and still-eyed way Kanye said it, the certainty of his special guest appearance barreling off the rails. He tumbled gracelessly into it, apprehensive but resolved to veer from the vaguely sentimental party-line script that Austin Powers had been so thickly attempting to play as sincere. There is a particular theater to public television. There is a particular theater to most everything furnished by the government.

The content of the telethon "was meant to subsume the racialized particularity of New Orleans's tragedy," to slyly erase "the hurricane's primary victims: black Americans." Except there was Kanye West, a celebrity appearance becoming a Black Person, right there on live TV for all of us to see.

It was messy because grief is messy. It was complex because the truth is. He's expected to say something along the lines of whatever passive and inoffensive text Myers read off the teleprompter, but instead he says, "I hate the way they portray us in the media." He gives examples. He confesses his own complicity. He states facts. He presents a logical conclusion. "You see a Black family, it says, 'They're looting.' You see a white family, it says, 'They're looking for food.'" The difference between an armed, calculating, and unremorseful white person, and a Black person armed with a vague suspiciousness that predates their birth. The difference between "no angel" and "troubled." The difference between execution and "police-involved shooting." (You really have to laugh at that one. You have to. Because otherwise . . .)

I often wonder about the conditions that create revolutions, what acts might be deemed revolutionary. How an average person, not otherwise a political actor, might be an agent of change. What does resistance look like on an individual scale, after the initial private moment of commitment to a cause? How does revolution emerge from the noise? Maybe it's as simple as interruption.

Rebellion against what is expected, acting outside the agreed-upon social norms. It's the citizen shouting, *I never agreed to this in the first place.* It's the citizen saying, *The rules don't apply.* In violating my rights, in ignoring my humanity, you have forfeited my respect for your structures of law and order. The government warns us that revolution breeds anarchy, that protest means riot. Both acts of revolution and acts of terror are disturbances: They seek to fuck shit up, to make people look. It is easy to claim that they are the same threat to safety and freedom. The government knows that the difference between revolution and terror is a thin piece of string, is a matter of rhetoric.

"HUMAN BEING"

My college therapist had a hoarse French accent that charmed and appealed to me. She was trained in feminist theory and gender studies, and I was newly released from a Christian school class of eighty and into something between *Gossip Girl* and *Igby Goes Down*. We talked easily about Lacan and Du Bois, and she gave me armfuls of old issues of *Poetry* magazine. I was a young poet, an anthropology student, in and out of various college identity crises, or alarming and ruinous depressive episodes, and smoking the most weed of my life. I was mostly concerned with surveillance, sex, and self-perception. It was an excellent fit.

I loved the tall plants and narrow book-lined hallways in her Riverside Drive apartment, its view of the Jersey skyline across the gray Hudson, and therapy in the Upper West Side felt like fulfillment of my destiny. And though I was starting to understand the importance of never showing it, I was romanced by all of it. The life I always said I wanted, the weather I longed to complain about, the rooms I could only dream of settling into.

When I moved across the country for college, I toyed with the idea of "reinventing" myself, but so much effort had already gone into crafting the self I'd brought with me. And though I'd been eager to abandon the belief systems that never felt like mine to begin with, I was ill-prepared to re-place them with anything other than a sharp rejection of where I'd come from, who I'd felt I had to be in the past.

I had been reading myself through the same filter for so long, measuring myself against the same unwavering and unforgiving white evangelical values, which required de-nouncement and rejection of any others. Yanked from the mayonnaise suburbs and into the diversity of Manhattan, and from who I thought I had to be into what I could choose for myself—much more than the usual freshman year exis-tential crisis awaited me. Having spent my life waiting to run away from my sheltered and prudish upbringing to the alluring and accepting opposite, I hadn't considered how provincial, lonely, and unfit I would feel once I arrived.

Even though I drank and smoked and cursed and pre-tended to forget Bible verses, the back of my mind still told me I was choosing hell. At least that was the word around town when I went home for the holidays, where nobody bothered with "happy holidays" because it was assumed ev-eryone celebrated Christmas. Everyone "experiments" in college; my revelation was that doing so wouldn't irreparably ruin both my life and afterlife.

The transition entailed more than finally studying evolution and having Jewish classmates, learning to be a "bad kid" without feeling like one, belittling my parents for their lack of knowledge on gender theory or labor politics, or getting my first B. While in high school I'd been embarrassed our family didn't regularly go to church, now I was embarrassed we ever had. Once, I'd calibrated wealth by whose house had a pool, not who had multiple houses.

"What will you tell your parents?" I'd asked my new friend at the Chase on the first floor of the student center, and he'd laughed, almost confused. "They don't check my bank account." My "rich" friends back home were broke compared to old-money heirs; they still had to buy their full-price Seven jeans with emergencies-only credit cards.

Recalibrating my sense of rules and decorum, my understanding of class and wealth, normalizing the regularity of mirrored trays of cocaine and friends whose parents padded their unmonitored bank accounts (while I'd call mine to atone for the extra forty dollars withdrawn for weed or concert tickets or accidentally expensive dinners off campus) weren't challenges for which I'd been consciously prepared. I knew I'd be behind, but assumed it'd be easier to catch up—because I was smart. I'd worked hard, and had unbridled ambition, and figured that was what had brought us all here—made us, in some ways, equal.

But while I was fluent in "secular" rock music and said *fuck* a lot, knew the classics were more than C. S. Lewis and the Bible more literary than law, I still hadn't been abroad. The East Coast came with its own class markers. I didn't know what it meant to be from Scarsdale, New York, or Greenwich, Connecticut. I wasn't familiar with the names of the most elite high schools of the Upper East Side or even more locally, in LA, or what it meant to be *a legacy*. It took me more than a semester to connect the drunkard down the hall in my dorm to the name on the building across college walk.

But I didn't want anyone to know that. For once, I wanted to belong where I wanted to, not where I needed to.

The rules of my roles, the politics of my status, had been made crystal clear in my upbringing. Consequences were simple: heaven and hell. All those years of my youth spent fine-tuning the appropriate mask to wear in front of white teachers and friends, decoding the best way to blend, the most protective. Now there was this whole other set of whites.

How could I introduce myself when I wasn't sure what myths needed correcting? How could I prove their expectations wrong when I didn't know what they were looking for when they looked at me? How is anybody supposed to operate that way, lacking so much information, without a clear understanding of the rules?

What I wanted to ask in therapy, what I couldn't articulate, was essentially a question of translation. What made people so comfortable, or afraid? How do others interpret what they see, and why? Grasping the perspective of one's audience is paramount to picking out your set. It's key to keeping safe.

English had been the obvious choice for a major—in fact I'd declared it in eleventh grade to assail any guilt for not advancing to statistics. I knew already that my job was to put words to things. But, as with many choices that would await me thereafter, there were far more options than I'd expected and a lot of words I didn't know. The description for anthropology glistened at me: "the study of human beings." Such deceptive simplicity. Under further investigation into the English course requirements, too, I discovered I had no interest in reading pre–1700 British Lit for an entire semester, and probably not at all. Studying human beings seemed more beneficial than an English major to becoming a writer. What in the fuck was a human being? The tagline seemed to sum up the underlying inquiry of my life.

The history of ethnography is inarguably the worst brand of white supremacist exploitation, as racist as the "scientific" measuring of our skulls, conceptualized and formalized by Western white men essentially going on safari and calling it fieldwork. ("How peculiar and bizarre the 'native' is! How mystical and elementary their ways of being!") Of course, the origin of anthropology also mirrors the history of psychology: pathologizing us as scientific practice. Gaining intimate access to hypothesize us, to make our wrongness official and provable. No wonder Black people don't go to therapy.

Columbia's departmental website currently states: "Anthropology examines the rooted concepts and everyday practices that provide frames for the ways people think, act, and make sense of the world (their own and that of others)." What were the frames and concepts that made me interpret intonations the way I did, made me insecure under certain gazes or unsure among others; and who had rooted them there? Did I worry, hide, overcompensate, exaggerate, or lust the way I did because of seeds planted in my mind, a bad-faith framing of my context? Which thoughts and impulses, if any, came "naturally" to me, were mine? How much of my identity was predetermined, if not predestined or purely constructed by invisible, historical forces? What would my instincts tell me, if I could hear them?

Processing all this as any college freshman might, I wrote a final paper about shifting concepts of the aesthetic sublime, Aldous Huxley's *The Doors of Perception*, and the use of hallucinogens in consciousness-expansion.

Obviously it had been a prelude to doing hallucinogenic mushrooms with a group of friends. We traipsed through the Santa Cruz woods, me scribbling field notes in my checkbook (the only paper on hand), and shouting, "I AM NOT A HUMAN BEING!" Throughout the afternoon, I'd tried to take off my clothes and roll in a patch of dirt, call my mom, call other people's moms, and talk to a bunch of strangers.

"YOU ARE NOT A HUMAN BEING!" I yelled at a guy sitting on a rock and strumming "Blackbird" on the acoustic guitar. Looking back, it makes a kind of sense, if you were to think of conscious questions as subconscious declarations: What is a human being?

After the trip, I made a pact with my therapist that I would consult her before doing psychedelics, to basically make sure my state of mind could withstand it—my mental illnesses had instilled a fear that states of terror might become permanent.

If my (Freudian-leaning) therapist wasn't trying to either steer everything to my sexuality or steer me out of debilitating depression, therapy sessions usually concerned identity and image. Even as I unloaded daily social and academic anxieties, it was about keeping up—with my own hopes for myself, with expectations of excellence, with who I was before and who I was becoming.

I felt abstracted, detached—like the world was too fast for me, and I was doing everything wrong. I couldn't get myself to feel like a perfect fit for anyone, any identity or lifestyle on the table. I was having intimacy issues with relationships and also general existence. With my family and past self on the opposite coast, how could I stay rooted? Who was I supposed to be?

When a Black sorority girl I befriended from my work-study job told me about a Black Student Union meeting, it was my therapist who encouraged me to go—and when she said, "Black people," she didn't squint.

In those years, Obama's hopeful smile was everywhere. Soon, we'd have a Black president; nobody knew yet what that meant or would mean for Blackness, the Black American identity—what, if anything, might shift in each of our daily self-perceptions and reception.

I didn't go to the BSU meeting. I'd planned to, even walked up to Hartley Hall a mere seventeen minutes late, saw all the brown smiling under warm light through the windows. The Black sorority girls with their flat irons and weaves, the southern Black churchgoers, the Black kids who grew up with other Black kids. Gathered together and looking at one another. I'd wanted to belong there.

Unfortunately I was more familiar with explaining my nightly headscarf to girls at the sleepover than not having to. I'd been the only Black person at the party plenty of times; I'd never been to an all-Black party that wasn't a family function and it would be several years before I would.

At the end of freshmen year, fed up with the humidity, I quit flat ironing forever and cut my hair off. At my high school, it would have been too Black. (I would have felt too Black?) At the Decemberists concert in American Apparel, I knew I still wasn't Black enough. When other Black people looked at me, saw me cackling with friends in the subway station, what was the tone of their *mm-mm-mm*?

Perhaps it's categorically narcissistic to think human beings could be figured out. I'm sure it's greenly idealistic to think that if we understood one another better, how and why we are, something could change.

I stayed with that psychiatrist for far too long, even after I moved to Brooklyn, three subway transfers away. Eventually I'd gotten so comfortable with her, I started to not tell her things. I wanted to impress or please her, so I'd leave things out or watercolor over them, like with a friend, or when doctors ask how many drinks you have a week. It had been something like seven years. She'd charged me the deeply discounted college rate the entire time.

She was my second real therapist, the first I had chosen for myself. After a session and a half with a counselor at the student health center, it had been clear her objective was to ascertain if I had "experimented" with "narcotics such as marijuana," and if I was on track for graduation. Even at eighteen I knew that wasn't what I needed, that moralizing my ache wouldn't be effective. At least not in the long run, which wasn't a possibility given the three-session max, and even at eighteen I knew that my depression wouldn't "go away" by dropping a course, that consistent talk therapy would always be part of my treatment. That at some point, if I was going to make it, I would need to trust someone.

In a way, it was the first time I felt allowed to articulate my psychological struggles in my own words. I could say my pain without fear of consequence or admonishment. Liberated from the pervasiveness of evangelical definitions of right and wrong, I could reframe my anxieties as more than an inability to "feel the spirit" and "be joyful always." "Right" wasn't just being palatable; "wrong" was no longer my birthright. My beliefs could be mine. I was possible.

WATCH HER RISE & REIGN

Southern California, 1998. I'm ten and it's almost summer, which means I have to go to my cousin Rhonda's to get braids. I don't want to. Everyone at school thinks braids are weird. Everyone at school is white. "Which is worse?" my mom asks: having to explain why I can't get in the water at the pool party, or having to explain what braids are? Both options make me cringe. When I taught all my friends the word "extensions," they wouldn't stop using it. Then when a stray braid was found near the library, it was like something out of a Hitchcock film: a crowd of white children wailing and pointing and laughing in a circle around me. My self-hatred became something palpable, something ugly and inadequate and all wrong. Everything about my life was embarrassing, especially the shame I felt about myself.

"The function, the very serious function of racism, is distraction," Toni Morrison said. "It keeps you explaining, over and over again, your reason for being." In practice, this distraction can take many forms. Why is your hair like that? Wait, you don't have any real hair? For me, a serious function of racism is embarrassment. I don't mean awkwardness—the fleeting moments that follow faux pas—I mean wanting to be erased.

Southern California, 1999. My dad calls me downstairs. Our family settles in on the couch, mesmerized. Two Black girls are on TV doing something important. They are winning, and they are Black girls with beads in their braids. They are Black girls from Compton, from just west of here, and there's their dad, doing what Black dads do—cupping the backs of their heads with his hands and bringing them in for a hug, urging them never to be anything but the best versions of themselves. Their smiles are the kind of smiles you earn.

I am famously unathletic—further proven during every recess and extracurricular activity, anytime I yearn to be part of a team. "Sports" is a world I'm excluded from comprehending, where my talents or insights are of no value. I don't feel any connection to the Mia Hamms and Kerri Strugs the girls at school idolize, and I'm not allowed to. I simply don't fit the profile of a champion. But I understand passion, and I understand grace. My burgeoning poet's brain is awestruck by the crisp sound of ball meeting racket, the liberal use of the word *love*, the way the players' bodies move through the air like comet tails. This is elegance, discipline, precision. I see myself. Take that, I think.

Serena Williams grows up and I grow up. I watch her rise and reign. Cosmically, it feels important to me that she exists in this world, persistently and reliably, holding her spot in her field as I stake a claim for myself in mine. She trains, I write, we grow up. They try to tug at the string of insecurity. They call us angry, crazy. They call us cocky, overweight. We have gotten too big for our britches, our Black dads would say. We can't help it if our ambition, our honesty and conviction, isn't what you want from us. They say our time is up. We act like it doesn't bother us.

New York, 2009. I don't want to get out of bed. I dodge calls from my therapist, who's only three blocks away from my dorm. I don't go to classes for a week. I feel burdensome and misunderstood. I'm embarrassed by my depression, that it is a constant fact of my life.

The New York Times says Serena has had a "meltdown," has an "aggressive demeanor" and "intimidating body language." They say she's unraveling, respect and class dripping off her like sweat. She later admits her battle with depression, and everywhere she looks there is scrutiny. Her language appalls them, frightens them, which is to say her personhood, her humanity, appalls them.

Poet Claudia Rankine describes the meltdown at the US Open finals as "a rage you recognize and have been taught to hold at a distance for your own good." It's familiar to us who have trespassed into professional worlds teeming with white people, worlds that depend upon your performance as respectable Negro, exceptional. Well-behaved. Serena's outburst, writes Rankine in *Citizen*, "suggests that all the injustice she has played through all the years of her illustrious career flashes before her and she decides to finally respond to all of it."

"What," she asks, "does a victorious or defeated black woman's body in a historically white space look like?"

What is incredible about Serena Williams is that everyone has stopped gawking at the irony of a Black girl from Compton with a tennis racket, and it's because she made them stop. The public waits for an opening, a slip-up, some justification to revoke her title, to make her into a nostalgic blip. But she doesn't give them the press bait. She doesn't hide in the bathroom wanting to disappear when she loses a braid in front of her white friends—she looks everyone in the eyes and says, "What?"

The world tells Black women to be embarrassed, in every language and on every court. About our hair, about our thighs, about our abilities, about our voices. Women are told to make themselves small and quiet. Black women are told that we're scary. That our emotions are a threat. If Black women listened to every voice in the stands, we would believe that as soon as we reveal ourselves to be human—to be vulnerable or opinionated rather than neat, elegant, demure—we become extinct. Audacity is choosing a different narrative. Deciding for ourselves what our victories will look like.

New York/Hell, 2016. The night Beyoncé drops *Lemonade* I am standing on a sidewalk downtown wondering whether to hail a cab or jump in front of one.

Days pass before I listen to the album. This is not my first time in Hell, being overtaken—and I am tired of it, standing at this figurative curb wondering over my worth. This time, I remind myself, finally—I want my life.

Days pass before my heart is able to see anything beautiful, before anything is worthy of celebration. But they do pass.

When Serena Williams shows up in a black-and-white frame of the breathtaking Kahlil Joseph–directed music video for "Sorry," I smile instantly. She is stunning, sparkling in a spandex bodysuit, and the combination of sex appeal and awe-inspiring strength in her thighs alone is almost scandalous. She twerks like there is no such thing as respectability. Her badass is a comfort. It's reassurance. She reminds me.

In black-and-white: Yoruba paint, daughters, esteem, a literal throne. Two Black women, wielding all their power, reveling in unabashed jubilation. *Sorry, I ain't sorry.*

In an interview with the Associated Press, Serena said that when Beyoncé asked her to cameo, "she told me that she just wants me to dance, like just be really free and just dance like nobody's looking and go all out. So that wasn't easy in the beginning, but then it got easier."

BROOKLYN, 2017. ON VALENTINE'S DAY, I RELEASE MY SECOND book, *There Are More Beautiful Things Than Beyoncé*, to a sold out audience at the Brooklyn Academy of Music. The rush of freedom I feel taking up the stage, looking back into the eager crowd, nourishes me in a way I never expected.

It is not a smooth ride growing into myself, accepting my success. Not because I'm afraid of failure, but because it's discordant with what the world typically accepts, with the role I was meant to play in relation to everyone else. Mostly white people.

With each praise accepted, each goal exceeded, I punish myself a little. Inextricable from any inch of accomplishment is the deep and shameful worry that I've gotten too big for my britches. Maybe that's why I feel so alienated, why people so readily blur me and Morgan Parker, conflate person and product. Maybe this is the catch—the price of unwarranted ambition, penance for success.

Visibility comes with its own invisibility, and a book tour is as exhausting as it is affirming. Offstage, the artist is faceless from city to city, necessarily dissociated from the aches and pains of personhood. You perform, you shake hands, and you are aware of the eyes on you, wanting. To be a Black woman on display is always complicated, always reminiscent.

Of course, everybody has an opinion about Beyoncé, and she comes up more than any poem. And of course, white hands always fly first into the air from the front row.

"But *are* there more beautiful things than Beyoncé?!?!" someone inevitably smirks, assuming they're the first to make the joke and not the eighty-fifth.

"Seriously, did you see *Lemonade*?"

Soon, I can't bring myself to laugh, to indulge even the most well-intentioned erasures. The mission of the book had been to celebrate and insist upon the multifariousness, the necessary complexity of Black womanhood. I don't have the words for how I am wounded by their religious fervor for a

Black woman—for what they have labeled "Black excellence," "Black girl magic"—what they have deemed our power and beauty, as ever, without our permission.

Black women aren't theoretical. That's what I want to say. What we feel and fulfill, our power and our pain—Is not theoretical. Is not as palatable as you want. We are not your punchlines, your queens, your projections. Looking into the crowd grinning, allowing my message to warp in their mouths, I suddenly become a minstrel. Whatever they choose to see.

There's a particular anger, Rankine explains, birthed from the stifling limitations placed upon us by the gaze of a white audience. We contain it, let the eyes fall where they may, keep rage tight in our jaws because if we do not, our anger will become a show.

What does anybody know about Beyoncé? What do we even know about ourselves?

As I bloom into performance, the already-slim possibility of real intimacy seems to shed petal by petal, and I'm increasingly afraid of my loneliness. Sometimes even I lose concern for lowercase me. Who cares about her, I figure. She's not who the people want.

SERENA WILLIAMS HAS FALLEN IN LOVE, SEEMINGLY OUT OF NO-where, she says. She never thought she'd get married. With her engagement ring and baby bump, she glows, and it's refreshing as California rain—to see her at the top, unequivocally adored and understood. Having it all. By now she's won practically every possible accolade and tournament in women's tennis, many of them several times, and shattered world records along the way.

"This is what I've always wanted," she says to HBO cameras, "since before tennis took over."

The Public Self obfuscates the private self, because that's what audiences want. They want to watch me confess my vulnerabilities—theirs—without the responsibility of concern for how it might strain my body, my heart, for the woman leaving the stage. They want to watch Serena perform, decontextualized from her anxieties about motherhood, the blood clots she fears might harm her pregnancy. They don't want to acknowledge they've built the pressure chamber where she dreads the inevitably harsh criticism of her late thirties comeback.

She thinks about settling in to married motherhood, daily swims in the pool of their Silicon Valley mansion, gifting herself simple enjoyments so long delayed—but she has too much to do. And she loves the game too much, so much she can't wait to touch her toes to the court again—as a mother, which is to say stronger than ever.

Soon after she learned of her pregnancy, Serena competed in the Australian Open—and won. By the time she was born, Olympia was living up to her name as a warrior goddess. Before she was born, she was already a champion.

The man-made, simulated battles of Black womanhood were designed to teach us to conspire against our own greatness, to call it accidental, to accept less and be only who we are told to be.

It isn't that Serena Williams is invincible, only that she understands boundaries are constructed so that we might be too embarrassed or obedient to cross them. She isn't a miracle; she has merely stepped into her own light, her own possibility, and gotten comfortable there. Of course we can be the best, be anything. Why should it be shameful or bold to say so? Why should pride and ambition be kept secret? What if self-assurance doesn't erase humility?

"I WROTE THIS FOR YOU," I SAY TO A STUDENT WITH A FEW PURPLE braids in her brown, and a tattoo that says "uppity negress."

In almost every book I sign, I write, "You are more beautiful than Beyoncé," and hope that as the book travels from nightstand to park bench to used bookshop, the reminder finds the Black women who need it.

One night I am reading in Georgia, where Tommy and I gasped at seeing our names in actual lights outside the legendary venue—which was once host to Nirvana, Iggy Pop, even my beloved Sonic Youth—and then smirked nervously at each other watching the pale audience members trickle in. Now every seat is full.

In the green room, where Cobain himself scrawled his signature, I consider changing my set in light of the lightness of the crowd, prepared for them to laugh at some of the right things and several of the wrong things. Tommy and I take our drinks onstage and ask for refills.

After lowering the mic I pause, bright lights blocking my

view from the stage, and shout to the audience, "Are there any Blacks?" I spot one, and maybe there's another I can't see. "Hey girl," I say into the mic. "I'm glad you're here."

SPORTING HER BABY BUMP ON SNAPCHAT, SERENA HAS THE SAME smile she did at seventeen. She's earned it, and she knows she deserves it. She's still here, where she's always been. We've grown up together and become more of ourselves, refusing the scripted roles. I put books into the world and I realize I'm not much different from the girl who sat at the lunch tables writing stories and poems. It can feel like no one expects Black women to survive—sometimes not even us. But even as rare as survival is, we don't have to settle for it.

When asked what she misses the most about playing, she says earnestly, "The crowds screaming my name."

Serena Williams has completely transformed the face of a sport traditionally reserved for white men in sweaters, and now I get to do the same for poetry. Wake it up. Serena reminds me that we can walk confidently through the boundaries. That we are worthy of being champions and worthy of being lovers—of being loved exactly as we are. We are worthy of anything we allow ourselves to have and we need not apologize for it. Incidentally, braids have made a miraculous comeback. I pile mine high atop my head like a trophy. I carry the weight with pride.

SELF
HELP

I've never read a self-help book before. I don't like when people tell me what to do, and I really hate when they're telling everyone else the same thing. Yet here I am, earnestly and soberly poring over a quiz in a self-help book about relationships, which I actually spent money on because I'm thirty-three years old and I've been single my entire life.

Not single "for a long time," but single forever, the whole time. *Single* may not even be the right word, because absence implies a memory of what once took its place. I'm single the way a baby is single.

By most sociocultural standards established since the beginning of time, my adult life could be viewed as inadequate and incomplete, if not tragic.

One thing about being unhappily single in your thirties—

besides the very real biological and social pressure to reproduce—is everybody thinks there must be a reason why. A reason that you must be somewhat content with or aware of, if you're taking no steps to improve your situation. As long as a person is unhappily single, there must be something wrong. You must need help.

Everyone has an opinion, whether I ask for it or not. Even strangers assume the authority to spit out armchair wisdom about what I need to do, acknowledge, let go of, how to get out of my comfort zone or "be open" or whatever. Because, of course, it's the task of the single person to receive and carry out any instruction from self-help books, magazines, friends, coworkers, mothers, people on buses, seminars, cab drivers, etc.

When it's not friends or Uber drivers with hollow clichés and prepackaged, one-size-fits-all advice, it's middle-aged businessmen at hotel bars or chatty randoms on airplanes with the gall to throw the question at me, shaking their heads like I'm a math problem. Sometimes it's people I'd hoped might be interested, men who would go on to kiss or sleep with me, and even those who'd already done so.

"Why are you single?" they press, in disbelief or suspicion, rattling off my many fantastic qualities.

Rarely am I speechless. But I never have a witty quip in response to this question, and the words *You tell me* feel like glass shards leaving my throat. "Slavery, white women," I replied once. Another time, on what I'd foolishly thought to be a date, I pressed my palms to the table and announced, "I believe I am the least desirable woman in America."

"I'm just not in a good place for a relationship right now," they say, before starting one with somebody else a week later. One such man lamented to me that he was an *anxious avoidant* personality. Usually, they're just hung up on their exes.

When white guys say it, I hate that I have to wonder if they're also trying to avoid the reality of actually having a Black girlfriend—bringing her home to the family in Maryland or Milwaukee; potentially adjusting the makeup of his social life; becoming compelled, as if possessed, to blurt out, "My girlfriend's Black," in defense, or as confession, explanation, excuse.

"You deserve someone better," they say. But "I'm not good enough for you" is just another way of making the rejection feel like my fault. No one answers the question.

I mentioned the *anxious avoidant* terminology to my psychiatrist, the one who's always telling me to go on dates, and she says something like, "Well, unfortunately, many young men who are artist types . . ." while wrinkling her nose and slowly shaking her head in disappointment. She recommended this book on "attachment styles" and explained how the authors suggest that people are either anxious, secure, or avoidant in relationships. She said I'm attracting the wrong attachment style. So I bought the self-help book and endeavored to read it.

I barely skim the intro, guiltlessly gliding over the authors' case studies about their friends—Pam's low self-esteem, Sam's obsession with his ex, Eli's boredom with his marriage—but when I read the bulleted list of each attach-ment style's tendencies, my throat drops to my stomach: Every column's unhealthy patterns and self-sabotaging be-haviors ring uncomfortably true. In lime-green pen I write *lol* next to a short paragraph on the "rare combination of at-tachment anxiety and avoidance," a category that "only a small percentage of the population falls into," because it de-scribes 99 percent of my dating pool, which consists mostly of artist types.

I KNOW WHAT YOU'RE THINKING.

"Have you tried the apps?"

Everyone offers examples of happily committed app users, sometimes including themselves. Even people who don't know what the apps are suggest I try the apps. People love the apps.

I created my first online dating profile fresh out of col-lege and, still hopeful, curled up on a curb-salvaged love seat in the funeral home for mice that was my Avenue C apart-ment. My roommate, who worked in fashion, told me it was an "instant confidence booster." After ten years and count-less starts and stops—including profiles ghostwritten by ex-pert friends and even a full-year premium membership at no small cost, albeit subscribed to by an accidental slip of the thumb—I've formally decided I hate the apps.

My thing about the apps: They make me feel terrible about myself. Like I'm back in middle school. Like I'm watching *The Bachelor* or whatever reality show it is, with all the white women standing in a line being desired. Like I've felt too many times before.

Once something becomes a cultural phenomenon—a mode of communication, an economic system—it begins to feel necessary, and not engaging with it means risking detachment or ostracization. For this and other reasons, including smoking bans on planes, I hate living when I do, and hope eternal for a more suitable placement in my next lifetime.

In order even to be considered eligible for courtship, you have to first be good at taking pictures of yourself on a phone, which projects your face back at you, taunting. You would be judged only by this snapshot of yourself, conveying just a hint of a personality—careful! not too much!—and a level of sex appeal on par with that of an "Instagram model," whatever that is.

It's not just that there's no smoking on planes, it's also those little pictures of cigarettes slashed through with a hard red line, glaring at me from every surface. How the reminder of restriction becomes the seed of craving.

I hate taking pictures of myself on my phone. I don't care to spend time staring back at myself in reverse, practicing a face. Instead, I'm good with words, and I've tried to develop my awkward version of in-person charm—what one reader called "a quirky and relatable vibe."

Vibes and words on dating profiles are secondary at best and might go unread entirely. There's no point in fretting over authenticity when most of the messages you receive just say, *Hey, how's your day going?* copied and pasted with no personalization or effort required, like being seduced by a greeting card that's blank inside.

The About Me doesn't matter because "bored, might delete" would perfectly suffice; and the standard template on both ends is little more than *I'm just a regular girl, I love music, food, and staying fit! Down for an afternoon hike and a craft beer?* ☺

Nothing against the regular girl, whom I probably know and love—and either way, she's by all cultural standards happier than I am. She gets to relax, check off the boxes of adulthood, certain of her worth and beauty.

When my Avenue C roommate purged her closet of outdated fashions, my side of the foldable clothing rack reaped the spoils. "Are you sure?" I asked as she gleefully dropped more hangers into my arms: blazers, sweater dresses, jumpsuits. Shoulder pads, she said, would never come back in style.

I'm not *just a regular girl.* I don't really want to be. But I want what she has, what she seems to so easily get.

The *Why are you single?* conundrum has sidled up easily to the shame I've felt about the ugly sides of my depression, which piggybacked nicely on the isolation of growing up a weird Black girl in a traditional white suburb. It's not like I needed any extra encouragement to discipline and punish my every flaw, everything that makes me different, anything that someone else might not like about me.

How would I act or even feel, were there no movies or self-help studies or think pieces teaching me how, teaching all of us the same *how*, telling us what to desire?

I'M A SCHOLAR OF MY SURFACE-LEVEL SELF-ESTEEM STUFF AND the African American self-esteem stuff, the consequences of an unconventional artist lifestyle, being *intimidating*, fearing commitment and abandonment and intimacy and rejection— basically all the fears. I understand my culpability and self-sabotage. (Additionally, it cannot be overstated how impactful the transatlantic slave trade and its resulting political and eco- nomic values has been in determining the results of my love life.)

After cycling through so many feelings of unworthiness and insecurity; scaling mountains of hard-won revelations about racism, gender performance, and triggers from child- hood; acknowledging my bitterness and letting go of hang- ups both interpersonal and sociopolitical, I've become more psychologically, emotionally, and physically available than ever before.

I've been Girl with Impossibly High Standards, Girl Who Puts Career First, Girl Who Self-Sabotages Out of Fear, Girl Who Needs to Love Herself First, and Girl Who Gets in Her Own Way, Girl with Unresolved Questions About Sexual- ity, Girl with Unhealthy Trauma-Based Defenses. I've lived and shed every rom-com protagonist's problems.

There's a cultural assumption that as soon as you've worked those things out, you find your person and start making a family/household/life. Until then, you're not ready and you're tasked with headbutting and knocking down each internal issue, no matter how much it hurts or how unfair it is that you must assess, Valentine's Day after Valentine's Day, what's wrong about your body or "energy" or psychology or vocabulary or life choices.

Surely not even half the people who've been in love have endured such extensive and unceasing analysis. It seems other people can quit critical self-assessment as soon as they're seriously partnered, and instead assume the authority to assess what's wrong with me and the choices I'm making. Unlike me, they have a piece of paper someone signed, promising not to freak out and leave when they're having a bad mental health day.

Before I've seen such commitment with my own eyes, how can I be sure it exists?

Until you've been in love, until you've had your heart broken, there's a large portion of popular culture that's sung at a pitch you can't hear. I can't sit through an episode of *Sex and the City* without spiraling into a fervent screed about expectations of femininity and pointing out oppressive value systems; I argue aloud with romance subplots, fuming, until every story is the story of what I am lacking.

Lately, even true crime pisses me off, because even serial killers on death row are managing to fall in love left and right. I can't stop thinking about how many chances for plots I've missed, and how I'd never wear that or put up with that, and that must be the reason I'm alone.

I went through high school without a boyfriend, college

without a boyfriend or girlfriend, my twenties without co-habitation or post-breakup Ben & Jerry's, no sloppy one-night stands at a bar in Williamsburg or a club on the Lower East Side turned into anything more. As years go by, narrative after narrative evades me; the possible storylines and adventures dwindle and little gasps of optimism deflate, and deflate, and deflate.

There is a difference between being single in your thirties and being "still single" in your thirties. Even I get turned off by restaurants on Seamless with no reviews and none of the stars colored in. Not worth the risk when there are so many other options with rave reviews and familiar names.

I know it's not like I missed my chance or anything, but part of me mourns the love stories that could have been.

What I mean is: I've grown up from a lonely girl into an alone woman.

THE ATTACHMENT STYLE QUIZ IS THE MAIN APPEAL OF THE SELF-help book for me, a former straight-A student happy to be given a tangible task, instead of "practice being more open." In spite of steadfast doubt that I'll be in any way transformed by the book's theories, I catch a gust of excitement at the prospect of righting the wrong of my style, the promise of becoming secure and even potentially attracting a secure person.

In chapters 3 and 4, the authors promise a two-step process for determining my attachment style and that of my partner. I skip the worksheet asking me to list examples from past relationships, and the whole chapter about the partner, triggered and ashamed that I can't even advance to step two. I sternly tell myself to discard the feeling that I'm automatically disqualified, beyond help.

My most comparable experience to real relationships are *situationships*. So, not nothing. But kind of nothing. I satisfy my sexual needs by waiting around for "hanging out" to turn into drunk, which then turns into "hooking up"—or, simply put, I have sex with my friends. Ours is a generation that thrives on vagueness, whatever gives us the most leeway in the end. We don't go on dates, we "hang out"; we avoid labels for as long as we can.

None of the authors' case studies depict someone in this label-less predicament, devoid of exes altogether. I scan my heart's memories, searching for any dalliance that might, with the right embellishment, suffice as data, at least for these purposes.

I've briefly entertained infrequent and ill-fated possibilities for romance, but one could convincingly classify all these instances as flings or one-night stands or some variation or combination thereof—flirtations I knew wouldn't work out but irrationally hoped might finally be my romantic storyline. Growing up I was the guys' "closest girl friend," first by default (as the less desirable option than the white girl), but then I realized there was little hope in escaping the platonic identity. At least I could delude myself into imagining a *Will-they-or-won't-they?* plot brewing three layers below reality. There are a lot of movies with romantic narratives like this, so probability-wise, the friend zone isn't the absolute worst place to hang out.

Situationships are just wax fruits in a bowl: They look like the real thing until you try to taste.

I TAKE THE ATTACHMENT STYLE QUIZ LIKE IT'S THE FUCKING SAT, reading and rereading every statement, hounding myself to be truthful (how much would I care if I saw my date checking out someone else, *really*?), counting and recounting and crossing things out. I even put it down and return to it days later with fresh eyes.

This is the kind of thing I choose to take seriously or assume that I must. With any luck, correctly calculating my score will illuminate the long-elusive question posed by men in my bed and kind old ladies alike: *Why are you still single?*

I'VE BEEN GENUINELY TRYING TO "BE OPEN" AND "PUT MYSELF out there." I go to bars alone like it's my job, and I even look around, resisting the glow of my phone and merely pretending to read. But what I've found is nobody is interested in looking at anyone, not right away, not by any means of effort. At least not at me. What I've found are people scrolling Tinder. In the bar. Right next to a single person. Never making contact, not even to say, *Hey, how's your day going?*

In real life, no handsome stranger reaches for the same

bell pepper in the produce section, no glances are exchanged in bookstore aisles, no martini appears "from the gentleman at the end of the bar." Everyone is terrible, and putting yourself out there actually means putting yourself into the phone, where someone might actually be looking.

IT'S A TIE: FIVE POINTS IN THE ANXIOUS CATEGORY, FIVE POINTS in secure. In the avoidant category, one point.

I BELIEVE MY SINGLENESS SHOULD BE CONSIDERED A COMMU-nity issue; that anyone who knows and regularly interacts with me should be as equally invested in my struggle-search for love. But since the apps became ubiquitous, nobody sets you up.

And though a lot of my friends met their person before app-based dating was seemingly the only option, it's the first thing they suggest. In fact, most of them have relationship histories already, and haven't been listening to this same song uninterrupted for three whole decades, so it's very frustrating that in a time of such peculiar crises as mine, they should have the gall to recommend something they wouldn't do in a million years. I know because occasionally I've responded to coupled friends' "you should try the apps" bullshit by indignantly thrusting my phone at them and have seen their faces as they toss it down on the table after just a few quick swipes.

It's much easier (read: effortless) to blurt the name of an

app you saw on a commercial than to ponder who might be eligible, let alone reach out to facilitate a setup. Personally, I wonder why they'd rather me meet a stranger on the internet with a one-line About Me, who could be a murderer or rapist or regular old white supremacist, than to suggest a mediocre date with a mediocre guy from their office mailroom. At least I'd know he's a proper human, and if I disappeared, they'd have a lead.

In our early twenties, singleness was a community issue. We took our responsibility as wingpersons moderately seriously, prioritizing locations where we might meet potential mates, scanning rooms, and doing a lap around the dance floor for prospects.

This is no longer the goal of the collective. It's just my problem. I am nobody's responsibility.

Something else about the apps: They're like a whole fucking part-time job. Apparently, you have to consistently put in several hours a week, otherwise you won't even show up on anybody's radar.

As if. I could write four whole books with all that time, and have.

Another game-changing storyline I missed is meeting someone before I became a "public figure" (i.e., on Wikipedia). As I chose poetry readings over clubs, blazers over party tops, I was aware on a surface level that I was guilty of "putting my career first" and risking prospects. I sort of expected to be in the musical-chairs conundrum I'm in, feeling like I missed an important window. But I didn't realize that by the time I was ready for a relationship, I wouldn't be just a "person" anymore, that I'd have another incarnation.

I do "put myself out there," everywhere, a lot. According to several unhelpful opinions, that's part of the problem. Flaunting a gregarious stage presence has done little to quash my problem of being "intimidating," feedback I first received at age twelve.

If you're an artist in front of an audience, your best bet is to take whatever you already are and make it extra, be yourself to the extreme. In dating, the opposite is advised. Apparently, you're not supposed to put it all out there at once. I find this vehemently counterintuitive, if not insulting.

It would be impossible for me to mind the traditional rules about stuff you're not supposed to say on a first date, since I say it all the time to audiences across the country. I'm just not in the habit of being demure or mysterious. What's the point of a slow reveal, if my whole job is going around talking about how sad I am, blowing off any opportunity to be coy or cutesy? I think that's why I find even the idea of dating boring. Who has the time to pretend to be one person, then hope your partner doesn't notice you slowly morphing into another, more complicated, and less shiny version?

In the absence of real intimacy, without proper experience or acceptance of it, I've practically professionalized vulnerability—to my assistance, and to my detriment.

To one of the standard OkCupid profile prompts, *The most private thing I'm willing to admit*, I answer, *is probably already accessible on the internet.* If you google me, one of the first things that comes up is a personal essay detailing how many antidepressants I take.

Sometimes, consoling or debating a potential-love-interest-in-my-imagination about his Actual Relationship, or anxieties or philosophy books or trauma, I'm aware that this guy's being someone he isn't or can't be with his current partner (who's usually of the Carefree White Girl variety). I wonder if that makes me immediately less desirable, not sexy—knowing them on that level. Being real.

I'm not the one they choose to make official. I've never been wanted enough to be. I've also, consciously or not, chosen not to be.

Both the problem and appeal of nonrelationship relationships is that they remove any responsibility from the deal. A foolhardy attempt to resist narrative and do away with the consequences of linearity.

Part of me is romanced by these terms. There is safety in clinging to the options of only wild and sticky, in being the one to make things difficult for myself before anybody else can.

You give: blow jobs, compliments, hours of unpaid emotional labor. You get what you get.

By now, my destructive patterns are obvious. It's easier for me to hear *no* and dismiss it than to wait for *yes*. Men tell me they're unavailable or unfit, yet obviously I pursue them, virtually begging them to make out as soon as "un-" is uttered, as soon as I know it won't work. Traditional, practical dating rituals are so much less interesting than the outcomes of wild, destined, and illuminating love, or the opportunity for more self-loathing and sticky emotional conundrums. Conventional dating practices might actually lead to something promising, and what then?

My primary skills of adulthood concern survival and salvage: cleaning up after my every innocent blunder; "figuring it out"; embodying man, woman, and child of the household. Flipping from one to another quicker than a code switch. To an extent, I'm incapable of imagining how I might fare or function in a couple. What if I'm too far behind, too embittered or untrusting?

I HAVE A GOOD LIFE. THOUGH IT'S CAUSED INORDINATE GRIEF in my daily existence, my continued and seasoned identity as Single Woman in this socioeconomic situation—as my life becomes more complicated and ambitious—has required me to get creative about my definitions of romance, of fulfillment, of growth. It's required me to reinterpret community and capacity. To be strong in surprising ways.

I am loved and cared for by a close family and warm, inspiring friends. I have my platonic "husbands"—a group of fourteen diverse in race, gender, orientation, and actual marital status—who've committed to me at least in title, and to whom I'm willing to commit and call my people. In the absence of the real thing, and because I've found it is necessary.

I see how it could be easy to overlook just how handy another person is. Just how many large or small gestures that make all the difference in avoiding misfortune: missed flights, that last drink, losing your phone (a bunch of times), keeping plants watered, getting somewhere on time. Not to mention affection and, frankly, regular sex. I'm certain that as a partnered woman I'd receive far more respect from strangers and especially Black elders. I'd be safer.

I was taught that "Miss" and "Ms." were placeholders until one grew up into "Mrs." Traditional American family value systems are always in the backs of our minds. Even when we insist they've been transcended, even if we pledge a life of defiance against them, they still define how things are "supposed to be."

The bylaws of American capitalism never meant for me, a descendant of slaves, to be a rights-holding citizen; or for me as a woman to be financially independent(ish). I've burst through several systemic barriers that should have left me dead or destitute by now. And in the same way, the social structure that adjusted itself to American capitalism is meant to favor the heteronormative patriarchal unit.

On a practical level, I'm less equipped than my cohabitating and committed peers to achieve the markers of successful and respectable adulthood—to meet all expectations without significant loss or charitable assistance. These are things I have a feeling my paired-off friends don't take into consideration when evaluating the appropriateness of my incessant despair. While you don't need a partner to be happy, coupledom is assumed to be an integral part of adult life and essential for anyone with too much ambition and not enough serotonin.

If, for example, I'm traveling as a Black woman with more than two suitcases, as I often am. If I forget to drink a glass of water all day. If two people are required for assembly. When sometimes, on tour in another city, I realize no other person in the world has any idea where I am or what I am doing, and nobody needs to. If I am so depressed I can't pull myself from bed to take the dog out. If I am depressed.

If I am depressed, and I think: Who would want this mess to bear? Why would anyone take this on, and wouldn't it be too much to ask of a co-parent, and would it even be responsible to reproduce or build a family, considering the hazard?

Sometimes, I'll just refuse to care for myself, in protest. Just to display how incapable I am, how unreasonable it is to expect one person to be so casually adept at so many things at the exact same time.

A TEXT NOTIFICATION SAYS THE NUMBER OF GUN OWNERS NA-tionally has doubled, and those who already had guns are buying more, many citing civil unrest and racial tensions as their inspiration.

The next alert tells me my OkCupid account has been deleted due to inactivity. I didn't even know that could happen.

THE PROBLEM IS TIME. IT SHOULDN'T MATTER, BUT IT DOES. TIME means regret. Regret means self-punishment. It's not just the general embarrassment of having the romantic subplot of my movie being introduced so late into act 2, it's also the close-fitting sense that time runs out faster for women like me.

What if I die before getting a look at myself in the bright mirror that is partnership, before tasting what everybody's talking about? Before finding somewhere to pour this devotion I've stored up, all this romance I've accumulated and dreamed? I'm a poet who's never experienced true romantic love; I believe this is an American tragedy.

When I go on strike against myself, nobody is there to see the display. No one rescues me, because I'm not a damsel. I can only care for myself by myself.

These days, stillness is the new hustle, the new collective goal. I'm just as tired as we all are, just as ready to exhale. I fantasize about moving to the Valley, a suburb outside the city—settling in to the aloneness I know so well, before it's too late to get comfortable at all.

Nobody wants a single artist living at the end of their suburban cul-de-sac, front porch blasting Fela in the morning and wafting weed smoke in the afternoon. Planned communities have no tables for one. Protection is built that way.

I am a thirty-three-year-old single Black female, self-employed, mentally ill, foulmouthed and politically radical. I can't move just anywhere. My safety is never in my control. My comfort isn't guaranteed.

While it doesn't invalidate my successes, the inability to achieve this one life goal—to "find love"—casts a little sorrow on the others. Even major achievements have a sour aftertaste. The more exciting things get, the more disappointed I am. Without a witness, a stakeholder, a rock—why bother?

If one is always in wait of one's Great Love, if every story depends upon this arc, how am I to be proud of the life I've created, who I've let myself become? When am I allowed to get comfortable, feel grown? If I choose to keep hoping for a romantic plot twist, does that render my story incomplete, still a pulsing cursor? And if I settle down, officially give up fretting over profile pages and wanting more from my flings and situations, would it be resignation?

Sometimes it hurts to think about, but then I just write another book, masturbate, cry, complain on Twitter, write another book.

I'm bored of being lonely. I've whined about it, gotten good at it, made it useful. I've learned and lived with my heart, the emotional sting of yearning. But there's still lack, and difficulty. There's still danger, everywhere.

The self-help book collects dust on a nightstand under an inspirational-type book from my other therapist, the one who's always telling me to "maybe just start thinking about possibly going on dates." We don't talk about loneliness anymore. Mostly, we talk about fear.

My life is a good one.

I don't want to keep it to myself.

UPENDED

In 2014, my therapist was this young, thin white woman who wasn't following the protests in Ferguson. "What's going on in Missouri?" she actually asked, after I told her how the city's summer swampiness felt thicker, airless, unbearable. There were few minutes that I hadn't been thinking about death, wasn't bombarded by it, didn't smell its perfume in every conversation and spontaneous panic, dread, mourning. The country was a tomb I walked around in, that we all did. It was the air, the weather.

Well remember, she said, I don't have a TV.

As if that were a conceivable explanation. So, before we can proceed any further in our session, where I'd hoped to continue discussing my desperate and unending loneliness etc., I have to tell her the story of eighteen-year-old Michael

Brown being shot and killed by a police officer, his body subsequently left lying in the street for four hours. I have to relay that protestors were being tear-gassed. That Michael Brown was unarmed and shot six times in the chest. She said that would explain the recent commotion in the park outside her apartment building in the Village.

Sessions with this therapist were tough, like a slightly patronizing Socratic debate or a bad round of charades. I stuttered, fidgeted, searched for my words, trying to translate between incomplete vocabularies. She very conspicuously took constant notes, to the point where she often asked me to slow down or stop so she could finish writing about me. There was an unsureness about her fidgeting—nervously pushing hair behind her ears, or tap-dancing her skinny heels on the tastefully unmemorable rug that covered the flooding gulf between us. One week, she wore red bottoms.

Those days I had to call my mom after sessions, or listlessly window-shop down Fifth Avenue, swallowing tears and letting myself be pushed around by the digital content producers and editorial assistants leaving their office buildings in the Flatiron. (These afternoons are how I discovered that the Gap is the best place to publicly cry in New York City—definitely better than the subway or Sephora. The employees are very accommodating and nonintrusive, and afterward you can get a practical and versatile basic as a souvenir or consolation—a crisp white button-down, socks printed with little watermelon wedges, a thing without a past.)

The summer of 2014 was death and grief and death and grief and litany and overture and coda.

My African Americanness became heavier; my country soured in my mouth. Everything felt like a joke, like a scientific experiment to see how much we could take. We talked about "calling in Black"—work and daily interactions seemed tedious, irrelevant. Unsafe, even. There was an epidemic of hopelessness, and an entire movement was created to advocate for the legitimacy of our very existences.

It was as if white friends blinked and there I was, Black, a reason to mourn. I got emails, texts, hugs, apologies from those who'd awoken. I never realized, they confessed as if to a priest, what you'd been going through. I hope I never made you feel this way—which left me with the responsibility to examine my remaining feelings. Or to articulate forgiveness? To cry or console? Either way, the catharsis and healing were not mine.

Mostly, I felt invisible, upended. No one had ever listened to us before. So many of us had to die before anyone stirred. Which meant so many more would have to die before anything changed.

SHE WAS MY LAST WHITE THERAPIST. IN HER OFFICE, NOTHING but the same watery questions with impossible answers. She is asking me to explain something to her, and I wish I could. *What does that loneliness feel like? Can you think of the first time you felt this loneliness?* Generations ago, I say. I laugh; she doesn't. She is asking me to point to what hurts. I want to tell her that I wear the past like heavy chain mail, that the ache is perpetual, that I never feel like myself. It takes effort to go outside. She keeps asking why. She actually says, *I don't understand.*

Did she feel any obligation, even curiosity? If for nothing else, then for the paychecks? She was responsible for help-ing me. It wasn't only that she didn't have the tools to fulfill her job, it was that she refused to admit she needed tools at all. That she asked me to believe that by the end of summer 2014, in Manhattan, as a mental health professional, she was unaware of the protests roiling nationwide over the fatal shooting of Mike Brown at the hands of the Ferguson police or the video of Eric Garner in a chokehold gasping his last breaths on a Staten Island sidewalk.

I started to miss sessions—I'd forget, or oversleep, or go get margaritas instead. I've spent enough time in therapy to know when I'm avoiding something, and to know it's not worth it to stay with a bad doctor. I wrote an email apologiz-ing for the missed sessions and explaining that "after think-ing about the pattern I have decided that I want to discontinue our treatment." While I was quick to add that she had been "immensely helpful," I expressed—very carefully—"that a better fit may be with a doctor who has a more similar cultural background." Here, I did not elaborate.

Then I threw in a second apology, for my "unprofession-alism" in missing so many appointments, as if I were writing to a work-study supervisor—and "any awkwardness in shar-ing this new realization." I sincerely hope to Nina Simone that breakups are not always this formal and penitent. I cringe now at how much I felt I had to give to her, how gentle I thought I needed to be. As if to be released, I needed to absolve her and be forever in her debt.

And anyway, I was paying her. This lady was one of my most expensive therapists—I was just out of financially reckless graduate school and working at a nonprofit then, so I'm sure many sessions were covered by money transfers from my parents—which was one of the reasons I broke it off; especially considering she was so annoying, and because I'd thought *I* should've been paid for explaining Ferguson to her. White women had started becoming insufferable to me.

She writes back. She thanks me for my email and agrees that the missed sessions have meaning. However, with regard to leaving her, she would like to learn more about how I arrived at this conclusion. She would like to offer me a free session to discuss "our ending" in person.

Maybe because it had the ring of an exit interview, or because of the idea of closure that people throw around, but I read the offer as a requirement, a demand, so I went. I do love a punchline. I did not look forward to the meeting, at which I'd had no idea what she or I would say, and I made plans to meet a friend directly afterward for margaritas— which was brilliant, because the exit interview was far worse than could have been imagined, worse than the job where I didn't have one.

She seemed to have an agenda, and she kept pressing, like I was avoiding some interrogation about my self-sabotage or whatever. What she chiefly wanted to know was what was it, specifically, that made me uncomfortable about discussing race with her, and had she offended me? She wanted to remind me that we had, in fact, talked about race, among a wide variety of topics. This is where it became combative and harsh. She'd asked me to talk more about race, remember? It had been me who couldn't open up to her. She wanted to know why I had only just now decided not to work with a white therapist. Why hadn't I said that from the beginning?

The question hurt. Whether I wanted it to or not, whether she meant it to or not, and whether or not it should have, the question rang as accusation and throbbed with power in my mind. I wasn't even Black enough to get a Black therapist in the first place. Had I never felt comfortable talking about my Blackness? Was I just faking the funk? Was I Black "all of a sudden," exploiting myself, making every little thing about race? These are the sorts of things you hear about yourself secondhand and from all sides. These are the sorts of things you hear and keep hearing.

I was not in therapy to talk about my Blackness, but because it's an integral part of my treatment for major depression. It's not like I could have anticipated August. But even later, at margaritas with Abba, I secretly told myself it was my fault I'd ended up here, with no therapist at all, with so many new fears and nowhere to voice them.

It wasn't exactly that white women were becoming insufferable to me, though I had very much grown tired of such moments as a white girl with an Audre Lorde tote bag bumping into me and saying she didn't realize I was even there. It was that their Facebook posts and downtrodden looks meant nothing to me, that sympathy felt pithy and, on the worst days, insulting. It was just that they were doing nothing but asking me to talk about my pain, explain, educate, and validate them and I had allowed this. But the slumber parties of my youth had ended, the university poetry workshops were over, and I was so tired. There is wear and tear involved in being observant.

Sometimes, when a white woman walks into a bar, I can guess where she will sit, where she will put her bag, how she'll pick up the menu. It's often against, or across, or from right in front of me without a word. She'll smile at me when it's too late. "Oh, I'm sorry, is this in your way?" when I've already gotten used to being entrapped by her belongings. "Oops, did I steal this from you?" when I've already asked for a new menu. She expects to be excused; I expect to excuse her. White women don't have to notice me, they think—the subtle messaging in my upturned lip, that I'm approaching on a skinny sidewalk, that I was clearly sitting here. Understanding the particulars of the daily life of a Black woman, what she wonders or prefers, what she fears or trusts, has no concrete bearing on their health or wealth and certainly not their mortality.

It wasn't that I thought white women were insufferable, but that their privilege was so loud, and its political power so glaring in my immediate vision that I could no longer accept their refusal to acknowledge it. Their apparent ignorance at how much is governed by their fears and desires. It was that their sympathies were so loud and their power so dangerous.

To recognize the reality of how different lives are is to

admit how violently corrupt reality is, the magnitude to which we refuse each other. What would it be like, particularly for white women, to make that a tool?

I spent a long time after that wondering about my last white therapist. The bold-faced gaslighting in how she chalked it up to not owning a TV. As if she'd never caught a TV in the corner of her eye at a bar, or mounted in the corner of a deli ceiling while waiting for her bagel; as if she never happened to glance at somebody's paper on the subway. As if she was actively refusing to gain knowledge of the world and its other inhabitants. The violent privilege of not seeing the news, not feeling the news in your muscles, not realizing the blood is in your water, too—which is to say, our fates are connected, because you said so. The luxury of living unaware of how your living might threaten someone else's, unconcerned with what dangers or consequences might befall you if it did. The comfort of knowing laws weren't written for you to follow so much as with you in mind.

Who did my therapist meet for dinner, drink with after a hard day at work? Did any one of them watch TV? Had none of them heard of what was going on in Missouri; and Cleveland; and Los Angeles; and Staten Island; and Beavercreek, Ohio; and Chicago; and Milwaukee; and Las Vegas; and Kansas City, Kansas; and Los Angeles again? Where did they live, I wonder, and how? Gramercy, or Brooklyn Heights, or somewhere else expensive and slightly nondescript? Were they everyone?

CODA:
AUGUST

Day 5. John Crawford browses a Walmart in Ohio. *He picks out a BB gun from the shelves, with the intent to purchase it. It's Tuesday. It is not a real gun. He chats on his cellphone, maybe asks his children's mother if she needs anything before he checks out. He's free, Black, twenty-two. Ohio is an open carry state, which is an American term meaning it is technically legal and vehemently defensible (i.e., not punishable by death) to be in possession of a firearm in public. A real one, licensed or unlicensed.*

Several other not-real guns are widely available in the store and in many other Walmart locations, though perhaps fellow shopper Ronald Ritchie didn't happen to pass through those aisles, or understand open carry, or know how realistic they make those things look these days, because he calls 911 when he sees Crawford, cellphone in one hand and the aforementioned toy in his other hand, who doesn't see Ritchie seeing him. And doesn't see when the two dispatched police approach and Officer Sean Williams shoots John Crawford to death. Another shopper, fleeing the murder scene, dies of a heart attack. The body count at Walmart in Ohio is two. It's Tuesday.

Four days later, outside St. Louis, they leave Michael to rot in the street.

Day 11. Ezell was my age. We would have been in the same class, were it not for sixty miles of California, and within years of each other we received our diagnoses. The medication he takes for his depression, bipolar, and schizophrenia makes him introverted. We're eighteen. I gain a little weight. Ezell is not affiliated with any gangs. Neighbors say his mental capacity was that of an eight- to ten-year-old, that his mental illness had become more noticeable since 2008, when he was a bystander victim of a gang-related shooting in his neighborhood of Florence, Los Angeles, where his family has resided for fifteen years. He wasn't all there, is what they say. Nobody knows to mention PTSD. The officers cried it was a gang area. The officers cried investigative stop. They were placed on paid leave. Three shots and Ezell Ford was gone.

Two days later, Michelle Cusseaux is fifty, then dead. She lived with mental illness, which is to say she had survived it, which means she had learned to ask for and accept help. Some days are beyond you. That's why her family and mental health workers had, on this Wednesday in Phoenix, Arizona, called the police for assistance. That's what they tell you to do.

Day 19. Back to Missouri. Mentally challenged twenty-five-

year-old Kajieme Powell wants to die, he says, holding a knife. Two responding officers swiftly comply with his wish.

*Williamsburg, Brooklyn, basement bar poetry reading, three PBR tallboys deep on the last leg of summer 2014. Before performing, I say to the audience—all white—*I don't know if you noticed all these Black boys getting killed, well I'm here to generate some white guilt for you ha ha ha. *It is quiet in Williamsburg, Brooklyn, at the end of summer and I laugh when I'm uncomfortable, when words are useless.*

In April it had been Dontre Hamilton, diagnosed with paranoid schizophrenia, shot by police fourteen times in under four seconds outside a Starbucks in Milwaukee, Wisconsin.

November would feel like August. Tanisha Anderson lives in Cleveland, Ohio, with bipolar disorder and schizophrenia until officers slam her head against pavement. Akai Gurley is an NYC public housing resident until an officer's "accidental discharge." Two days later, on November 22, two grown officers in Cleveland kill a twelve-year-old boy playing in the park and they call that an accident, too. Still we are told to give thanks.

PLANTATIONS

1.

The day I go to the plantation is the day the rest of the group goes kayaking. This makes sense to everybody.

When my friend Julie invited me to give the keynote speech at a writing workshop in Bradenton, Florida, I googled the city. What these types of gigs lack in consummate funds, they usually make up for in quality drinking time with writer friends I too rarely see, and sometimes they're in odd places I'd otherwise never have reason to visit. If I'm lucky, it's somewhere jazz funk records and first edition poetry books are grossly undervalued, aplenty, and marked way down. In Indiana, I bought so many books I had to ship them home. In Kansas, I loaded up on Black music from a bargain bin. In Portland, it was Richard Pryor LPs (only five bucks each?!).

Maybe there's a museum exhibit in town or a local natural wonder. This city had none of those things. But it had the only surviving plantation in south Florida.

The Gamble Plantation was rescued and gifted to the state by the United Daughters of the Confederacy in 1925, and in 1970 the "Robert Gamble House" debuted on the National Register of Historic Places. It's also referred to as the Gamble Plantation Historic State Park or the "Gamble Mansion," and Wikipedia describes it as a "forced-labor farm"—but I double-checked, and indeed the Robert Gamble House was simply a sugarcane plantation that held over two hundred slaves during its peak.

My people aren't from Florida, at least I don't think so, but a plantation is a plantation. Anything to get me closer to myself. The mammy saltshakers that speckle my apartment, *The Black Joke Book* and its slurs tucked deep in my shelves, anything to remind me of the history of how I've been seen. Today I feel more like going to the movies or a greasy-spoon diner, but it's our free day, my only chance to go. Not like there's a "better mood" to be in for a day at the plantation.

When I arrive there's a tour finishing up, so I'm encouraged to browse the exhibit. The lobby "museum" is skeletal—a sword here, a posterboard there—and I remember that it's for the house itself rather than the events associated with its existence. The display boxes showcase numerous tools used in the building of the home, architectural plans, details about sugar cultivation, a diagram of a water filtration system. When I finally spot mention of slaves, the matter-of-fact text explains how their labor was used. On my second lap through, I snap cellphone pictures of the few paragraphs about the Seminole Natives "sometimes viewed as a threat," prompting Gamble to arm his slaves for battle against the land's former inhabitants. I double back for a close-up of the plantation's first inventory list of 142 names, all of them pseudonyms for slaves, the last of which is identified as "an infant child of Adeline."

Outside, I wander a patch of the plantation's remaining sixteen acres and make the mistake of looking up at the willow trees. I am standing where slaves stood and swung. I tell myself I won't do that with every step—retrace, flicker back, remember. But looking at the trees in their weeping, it's like I'm carrying more memories than I have.

I think about seeing the same willow tree every day, how it might feel to pass these branches daily and remember the last body, remember how branches are used. How it might feel to watch a regal willow slowly grow outside your window and know even their beauty has been robbed from you, stained.

I am the only one on my tour. My guide is an enthusiastic middle-aged white man, who asks me to sway in the porch's rocking chair while he begins his presentation. It should have been a wailing clue about the tour's perspective and therefore its tone altogether. My hint I didn't belong there. The second time he asks, I comply.

The antebellum house is fitted with obnoxious Roman columns and fashioned in the "Doric Revivalist vernacular architecture style," which is to say it reeks of ego. I find it tacky—its exterior so deeply discordant with its personality. Who does Robert Gamble think he is?

I blink at the sun while the guide recites his spiel as practiced. He asks me to imagine "living back then, looking out onto your land on a warm afternoon like this one."

I'm still a little hungover, I'm realizing. My wise-cracking muscle is sluggish. Another day, here would begin a multitude of under-breath quips and dark jokes tumbling out of me, making both of us wonderfully uncomfortable, maybe eventually loosening him up for an interesting conversation. I definitely do something—maybe I cock my head, snort, or make a face—to address the obvious discord, my invitation to lift the pretense—a request, really.

But even though I am the only audience, he continues on this way. Second person. Putting me in the master's shoes.

The tour covers mainly two phenomena of the Gamble Plantation: that it was built by Robert Gamble and his "workers" using a moderately nontraditional material called "tabby"—a mix of sand, limestone, and oyster shells—and that it harbored fugitive Confederate General Judah P. Benjamin after the Civil War, aiding his escape to England via the Bahamas.

We talk about tabby at length—I can't stress enough how in-depth the tabby segment was. Finally inside, we tour a sitting area furnished with colonial artifacts, a spare, sunfilled room with an "era-appropriate" writing desk. None of the furniture is original, but it is "period," so unfortunately I have to politely nod through a bit about that stuff, chairs and carpentry. In the dining room, the table is fully set with delicate china dishware. This is where Gamble entertained, my guide tells me, pointing at a decorative tea caddy much like those prepared by "the staff" for Gamble and his guests. I keep my mouth shut.

Major Robert Gamble was a rich kid who got the plantation's acres for free. Following the Second Seminole War, after forcibly removing Native American families from their land (and calling it destiny), the government instated the Armed Occupation Act just to make sure the displacement was speedy and permanent—a whites-only free giveaway of the stolen Native land, including the 160 acres where Gamble, a bachelor, built his tacky ten-room house.

I keep waiting for the tour guide to say "slaves."

Upstairs, in the bedroom, we pause in front of some formal portraits—guys with George Washington hair and Thomas Jefferson ponytails—and the guide points up to a porthole window across from the bed. This gave Judah P. Benjamin a clear view out to the Manatee River, he tells me, so he could see any Union soldiers coming to capture him.

Former US Senator Benjamin, who himself owned more than 140 slaves on a New Orleans sugarcane plantation and was known for the eloquence of his proslavery writings and speeches, held three different major cabinet positions under his friend Jefferson Davis's confederacy. After the Union victory, he successfully fled capture in what *The New York Times* purportedly referred to as a mythical escape from Florida. Benjamin begins his Odyssean caper in Georgia disguised as a traveling Frenchman, makes his way through

Florida posing as a farmer, hides out in the homes of prominent families outside Tampa, who secret him to the Gamble
house near Sarasota, where a boat would smuggle him safely
off the continent. He sailed to Bimini, traveling through the
Bahamas and finally to London where he settled, almost immediately gaining acclaim and admiration from the law
community.

Judah P. Benjamin went on to a long, lustrous career in
England as a member of the elite Queen's Counsel and the
author of a book on property law that continues to be widely
taught in the United Kingdom and the United States. He'd
been a prominent lawyer and politician before the Civil War,
and was a prominent lawyer and politician after the war. No
trial for treason, no new identity, no shame. Like moving out
of state after a bad marriage.

They always have somewhere to hide. Nazi doctors,
criminal presidents, heads of bankrupt hedge funds. In the
rubble of the revolution, when everything must be faced
and changed, they're allowed to get lost, wriggle themselves
from the arms of accountability.

It's masterful the way the tour is not about the Civil War
at all, that its years are described as "period" or "prewar era,"
its circumstances simply framed as a time of candlesticks
and hand-carved chairs. Other than the "close call" when the
home's owner spotted Union troops coming for Benjamin,
and the pair snuck out the back just in time to disappear
into the trees and avoid capture, my guide relays little to no
conflict. As he lights up narrating the salivating tales of the

hero war criminal's triumphant escape, I realize I'm supposed to be impressed.

Robert Gamble was a bachelor, the guide reminds me.
Never took a wife. I catch my breath a little, aching for the
Black women alone with him there on those remote acres.
If he was drunk. When all the guests had gone home. If he
decided he wanted to take something.

Gamble more than doubled his number of slaves over
the course of the plantation's operation. After only twelve
years, sunken into debt and disgrace, he lost it to creditors.

The bedroom spiel is mostly about the inconveniences of
colonial life, similar to the one I received at Knott's Berry
Farm in fourth grade, when we learned to churn butter. *They
didn't have what we have.* No central air or heat, no night-
lights, my tour guide says, displaying a chamber pot for piss-
ing. Many preparations went into bedtime. Oil lamps, coal
for the furnace, mosquito nets in summer. The house staff
went up long before Gamble and guests to ready the un-
sophisticated feather beds, which were lumpy and needed
to be plumped and smoothed manually each night.

On the four-poster bed is a "period" quilt and a large
rounded paddle, the presence of which I'd definitely mis-
taken for a whip upon entering the room. He picks it up to
display.

"They'd get the mattress nice and smooth, so you could
get a good night's sleep!"

"Well, not me," I blurt, and my hurt-feelings laugh slips
out. The man doesn't respond, just continues to smile

blankly, politely, like he doesn't understand, like he's the first truly color-blind white American, or at least the most cowardly.

I didn't have to laugh. That had been a gift to him.

There are no slave quarters on the Gamble Mansion Historic State Park. "They would have been out thereabouts"— he gestures past some picnic tables, toward the jungle of unkempt oaks beyond the house as we head into the kitchen— "but this is where the staff worked all day."

"The slaves," I say, and he nods, pointing me toward a loom.

Everything had to be handmade, he reminds me. Clothes, coffee. He goes, "Say Robert Gamble wants a cup of coffee," and walks me through the laborious steps of heating the oven, roasting and grinding beans and chicory. I am still thinking of the memories of the female slaves, the "staff" at the behest of Major Robert Gamble Jr., the war hero who bought land for cheap to own hundreds of people and entertain guests in a ten-room McMansion for barely a decade before moving on to something and some bodies else.

We step back out into the sun. It's warm, especially for January, and I slide on my sunglasses, impatient, as the guide leads me to the plantation's freshwater source, a swimming-pool-sized covered cistern on the side of the house, where he gives me an extensive presentation on its functions and maintenance, its gallon capacity and drainage system. As he summarizes the plaques on the old dinner bell and cane roller, preserved among ruins of the sugar mill, I notice just beyond, two women in corporate slacks and lanyards having lunch.

When the United Daughters of the Confederacy bought the property, restored the plantation into a mansion and re-branded it as a historic state park, they also bought the scope and subject of its preservation. They added a memorial headstone for Confederate veterans. No period slave cabins were reconstructed. They added a decorative archway for weddings. They added a picnic area with grills. They pre-served the work room.

I don't provide additional quips or commentary for the remainder of the tour. And it hadn't been as rife with mate-rial or emotional terrain as I'd wanted. The ratio of time spent on tabby versus anything else was frankly absurd to me. The tour had been technical almost—more about the mechanics and structural materials than any inhabitants. Engineering, not experiences. The slaves—me—were farm tools, conduits of conveniences. There were no souls pres-ent, conjured or evoked. There had been facts but no infor-mation.

When we conclude, I just think, this guy has no idea what I see when I look at the willow trees.

For the tour, I paid six dollars.

2.

After touring the Robert Gamble Plantation, I try every other available direction and storefront in my sight line, deliberately determined to avoid going to Popeyes. As soon as my Lyft driver's monster truck had pulled up to the mansion gates, and I saw the Popeyes directly across the street, I'd made a pact with myself not to go there, even though I was already hungry.

But now, it was closing in on evening, and all I had in my stomach was a chalky Coke to ease my hangover, which meant I hadn't taken my pills, which meant many things, but mostly, I needed to eat food. Bradenton, Florida, is not a walkable city, nor is the area surrounding the Historic Memorial State Park aka Plantation a "neighborhood." I hobble in my clogs over rocky pathways and dodge traffic across the highway. In the distance, at the next corner, maybe a gas station? When I get there I see two Florida men scowling at the entrance to an auto garage and only then do I make my way back to Popeyes, where I loiter for fifteen more minutes, searching "food" in Google Maps, coming up with nothing but shopping center sandwich shops several miles away. And so I find myself, an African American, sitting in a Popeyes, looking out at a plantation, refusing on principle not to try the raved-about chicken sandwich, swallowing down a capful of antidepressants.

You can see the Popeyes from the Big House. When my tour guide waved his hand gesturing out past the gates, down the few streets to the water where slave ships docked, its poppy-red neon sign was center frame. "All of this was clear, just marshes," he'd told me. "They could see if enemies were coming." From here, one table away from an elderly couple sharing a sandwich, with drive-thru orders as white noise, it looks like a state park. They preserved their leisure. Who picnics at a plantation?

There is no way to make the cardboard container of breaded and fried chicken tenders appetizing in this moment. It's all too much, too many layers to digest—the juxtaposition of iconography and the forced conversation between two vestiges of the slave trade, two landmarks illustrating the economic legacy of African America, two buildings painted with exploitation.

At Popeyes I wonder who picnics at a plantation and I wonder if I am doing the same thing.

A BALE
OF
COTTON,
FOR
EXAMPLE

In my notes for this book, I incorrectly wrote down the following sentence from *Black Rage*, written by psychiatrists William H. Grier and Price M. Cobbs in 1968: "The black [person] of today is at one end of a psychological continuum which reaches back in time to [their] enslaved ancestors." I'd accidentally left out the words *in time*—I guess subconsciously and otherwise, this is how I prefer to think of things. I don't believe time is only linear, and I don't believe I haven't known this world before.

As a measurement, time is culturally relative. We decide on it, delineating zones and establishing schedules even as the moon wanes and dictates above us. We claim progression even as bills are reversed. We praise innovation from the rubble of our destruction.

Neither history nor memory really benefits from or reflects the structure of linear time. It's just that a particular economic system depends on a particular definition of evolution, demands a linear measurement of what matters. Our concept of *forward* determines what is of import. What is matter, filling waters and coffins and buses and ships.

Evolution implies directionality, the chokehold of having only the two options—forward and back. The constraint of verticality between origin and resting place, enlightenment and punishment. Afrofuturism upholds one linear end, and the bottom of the ocean, Ralph Ellison's invisibility, and the "sunken place" of *Get Out*, take residence at the other end.

Who gets to decide which direction we evolve in, what becomes obsolete, which behaviors are pathological? The internet, the hedge funds, the banks, the elected officials, the alignments of planets in orbit? Who says we're going in the right direction?

IN HIS MEMOIR, *PRISONER OF LOVE*, JEAN GENET WRITES: "IN White America the Blacks are the characters in which history is written. They are the ink that gives the white page a meaning."

If we are only characters in the American drama, if we're the stage where America dances, then our own history is subsumed in our role and function in the American narrative. What does it mean to have "history," "culture" written on oneself? Or—what, then, is the self, and what is the weight and responsibility of it? What task comes with being born into so much unshakable, undecipherable weight, re-born into it daily?

Artist Glenn Ligon refashions the quote in his text-based piece, "Prisoner of Love #1 (Second Version)": *We are the ink that gives the white page a meaning.*

Owning history means owning perception and potential. The facts. What people think about themselves. What if all I believed about my past was what I've been told about my past?

Black Americans are groomed for gaslighting from our very beginnings, sometimes to the degree that the very concept of fact seems colonialist. We're gaslit in the tradition of the Fugitive Slave Act and the three-fifths compromise. We are gaslit in the American tradition that forced new names on us, the same names we have today. We're told our pain isn't real, our grievances too old or unproven. Even science says we're ugly and stupid. Truth feels like a scam when your self-development depends upon dispelling the ones you've been told. Every day that I write my name I remember where it came from.

It's hard to trust and affirm the instruction and explanation of the same whiteness that convinced me to hate myself. To pledge pride in a country governed by the same laws written under the auspices of my enslavement, rape, and torture; by the same document where I am not included with "all" but am included under "property"; and by men who would die before writing a new one. Why should the rules of government, and its rhetoric, apply to us?

The audacity of our continuance, the defiance of our

physicality in this country, proves there are different laws and limits for different bodies. "The citizenship of the Negro in this country is a fiction," historian Carter G. Woodson begins his 1921 essay "Fifty Years of Negro Citizenship as Qualified by the United States Supreme Court." Why uphold such a lie, he asks, when we can plainly see the Constitution disregarded or otherwise not applied to us, when, "despite the unusual power of the Federal Government"—to declare and end wars, collect taxes, and coin money—they've "studiously evaded the duty of safeguarding the rights of the Negro." After Emancipation, the Supreme Court's function conveniently shifted from "preserving the Constitution by democratic interpretations" to "easily disclaim[ing] jurisdiction where human rights are involved in cases in which Negroes happen to be the complainants."

In the years before the Civil War, before even fictional citizenship was on the table, proslavery pastor George Dod Armstrong used US law as swiftly and confidently as biblical scripture, calling into legal question our very humanity. He quotes, "'Slaves shall be claimed, held, taken, reputed, and adjudged in law to be chattels personal in the hands of their owners and possessors,' is the language of the law in South Carolina. And hence it is inferred," he reasons, delicate and technical, "that law does not regard a slave as a human being, but as a '*thing*.' If this be the correct view of the case, how comes it that the laws in South Carolina make the killing of a slave, murder; and the forcible violation of the person of a female slave, rape? Can a 'thing'—a bale of cotton, for example—be murdered?"

I can't believe in history because I want to believe in progress. I can't believe linear time because no matter what year it is, it's the worst year to be Black in America. That's what I mean when I say facts are white.

When I insist to a white friend now that "I was on the slave ship," that I remember it in ancestral flashbacks, when I name it Trauma, when I argue about the delineation of past and present—it isn't just that he doesn't understand, it's that the "rules" are on his side to say otherwise. When I tell white friends I know it, I experience it, and they feel no adjacent complicity or ancestral guilt, they actually have the perfect argument against me, and I've given it to them. They have rhetoric, "fact," and they have it at the ready, sometimes before I've even finished what I'm saying, which they can then push away without absorbing. "You never picked any cotton." "You're from suburban California." "You weren't even born."

They have evidence: Every time I've held my tongue. In all the nineties sitcoms, for all of their Gap commercial diversity, the third act of an episode always proved the Black character wrong if they had suspected racism. That was the lesson—don't be paranoid, that's not cool. That was then, it happened to somebody else.

"INVISIBILITY," SAYS THE NARRATOR OF RALPH ELLISON'S *Invisible Man,* "gives one a slightly different sense of time." Offbeat, he says. "You are aware of its nodes, those points where time stands still or from which it leaps ahead."

Time stopped for us on the boat. Something froze, and something else moved forward, and we carry both. We still have the selves that were lost there, under the water, in the glitch of the slave ship. "It began with slavery," write Grier and Cobbs in *Black Rage*, "and with a rupture of continuity and annihilation of the past." They write, "There is a timeless quality to the unconscious which transforms yesterday into today." The unconscious remembers and the unconscious collapses.

How could we not conflate an unarmed shooting with the tossing overboard of African women and children as excessive cargo? The debate over whether our lives "matter" and the Dred Scott decision? How could we believe these events to be relegated to a vague, thorny past, to believe them events at all, as instances instead of a condition— something regenerating and perpetuating, nodes of one moment.

Poet, essayist, and activist June Jordan wrote that Black America embodies the extreme "questions of freedom and identity: *How can I be who I am?*" Not: *Who am I?* I think it's important there's a verb involved, that the question of existence is welded with the question of allowable action. Not how can I be, but how I can be myself. She writes, "we mean to rescue the person from the amorality of time and science." The amorality of time claiming to be linear, and science sending our bodies to zoos. We mean to rescue personhood from the boat—rescue the person from the damage incurred in the rupture.

"Colored people time," however its roots have been cut

or rotted, is an homage to our pre–American Black sensibilities. Getting there when you get there. Going home when the court lights come on. When I asked my mom my birth time, she told me *a little bit before dinnertime*, so I filled out forms and wrote a check to get an official copy of my birth records. If the astrological implications of an exact time stamp weren't important to me, it would have been a waste of money. I was born at 4:23 P.M. We tell time how we need to. When we say tomorrow, we mean a whole lot more than that.

I'll never have what I crave the most: a charted map, lights on the trail of events that got to me. Something to stand on. So instead, I stand next to. That's part of what I mean about linear time. Other planes. Living history— rewriting and prewriting history because history was written without our consent.

"The consequences of Black miracle in white America:" writes Jordan, "All of us hunt identity."

WHILE WORKING ON THIS BOOK I KEEP MISREMEMBERING A LINE from Saidiya Hartman's *Lose Your Mother*: "The most universal definition of a slave is a stranger." It rings in my head as *useful*. The most *useful* definition. The most useful definition of a slave is a stranger.

Maybe because of the way our transport and transformation from there to here is so tied to our use, as in the usefulness of our effort and energy. In making the trade from human body into product, our bodies were also rebranded as labor.

Not only did arrival onto the boat mark our transfer from person to property, relabeling our bodies, it also (re)defined how our bodies would be used. And who would use them.

"The slave defines the position of the outsider," Hartman writes. "Africans did not sell their brothers and sisters into slavery, they sold strangers."

Labor, by the way, is a verb. Yesterday, I was a proper noun. Our new "identity" came with new rules, tasks, and limitations. The vastness of the boat is how it robbed not only our identities but our actions, too: what we're allowed to do with our bodies, including but not limited to where we're allowed to go in them and how far.

Editor Floyd D. Barbour wrote, in 1970, "In between is repetition and counterpoint. If repetition has a meaning, the meaning is force, and force is what brings down barricades! Repetition, like the individual frames of a strip of film, is always changing." A lot of things work like poetry: With each repetition the word ignites a new feeling. "The question remains:" he continued, "will there be a change even with all the repeating?"

The slave ship as motif: a static painting changing frames. Force: what moves the waves under the ship. *Force* is both violent and propulsive. Force could mean the plantation and the revolution.

This is what I know for sure about my ancestry: It started on a boat. Our African American journey, culture, and memory—it starts somewhere there, between, on the boat. It is an otherworldly place, a node of time, a site of confusion and war, and, like the African American identity;

full of possibility. "No one on earth ever had a greater chance for glory," Zora Neale Hurston wrote. Because there is also a repetition of our resilience and humor, our inventiveness and continued search for what *freedom* looks like, could be, and betta must be. *That's what you hear vaguely*, says the Invisible Man, *in Louis' music*.

The boat is just a name I use for the glorious complexity and estrangement we carry and fight about and joke about. A name for an origin and legacy. I trace back to *yesterday* with curiosity about today, to retrace the steps toward present. I trace backward knowing how much I will never uncover or retrieve, but I look back with hope of repairing some damage incurred on the journey here.

If you are alive on the slave ship, revolt is still possible. If you are alive on the plantation, escape is still possible. If you can breathe, you can.

DIASPORA BEGINS AT HOME

I n the opening lines of Zora Neale Hurston's autobiography, *Dust Tracks on a Road*, she writes: "Like the dead-seeming, cold rocks, I have memories within that came out of the material that went to make me. Time and place have had their say." To understand her, she insists, you have to understand where she came from, what time and place has said about her. Her birth doesn't happen until the third chapter, which begins: "This is all hear-say." Which is usually better than the truth, anyway, and certainly more interesting. And which, for most of us, is basically all we get. All we have to work with.

Though white people may feel permitted to see it as a casual inquiry, "Where are you from?" is a weighted, challenging question. The cruel half of the punchline is how they don't see the irony—that they'd know better than I would, that their ancestors took my answer and dumped it at sea like a corpse, that their lineage is the reason I only know so much about mine, why I can only see so far back. "You tell me" would only cut my throat coming up.

It's hard not to hear it like they're mocking us. I always feel disappointed in myself when I don't know the answer. Especially when I should.

I have Black friends from such places as Chicago and New Orleans and the Bronx, and I have watched them draw tears arguing about which city is more authentically Black, which cultural terrain and twang held the soul womb of African Americanness. And they all had good arguments: centuries of historical significance, ancestral roots leading back to African rituals and tongues, early communities of free Blacks, who got here first, and what America sees when they picture Blackness. I could argue on behalf of nowhere. No Black pride was built into the landscape of Southern California suburbia—planned communities designed for those who fled authentic Black cities, who did not want to see color. But of course there are Blacks, and there is Blackness, in the west. We're one of those kinds of plants that can grow after they've been cut from the root.

In Amsterdam that day, with our group of Black writers from the United States, we'd learned the history of the city's Black community, most of them descendants of slaves from Suriname, the Caribbean plantation colony where Dutch traders dropped off their African goods. We'd viewed archives of anti-Black Dutch media, letters between Black

Dutch and Black American revolutionaries, the ornate homes of slave traders. We'd toured unmarked reminders of Surinamese genocide, the former headquarters of the Dutch West India Company where the first stocks were traded and some of the first slaves sold.

We had come to the literary festival, some of us strangers to one another, as the Black Americans: harbingers and ambassadors of American Blackness to our diasporic counterpart, Black writers from the Netherlands. The intercultural conversations had been complicated and thrilling, but the factioning and friction between us Black Americans was exhausting and overcomplicated. What was everybody trying to prove? It wasn't, however, unfamiliar.

When a short "agree to disagree" lull befell the table, I said, "I think sometimes people forget about us in the west." To my surprise, they admitted it. There had been the Panthers, Rodney King, I guess, sure, we think about that.

"What does that mean for my Blackness?" For Black kids in Orange County or San Diego, pockets of suburban Arizona or small-town Nevada? Were we inauthentic by reason of geography, just accents and add-ons to the Black American cultural tableau?

I have never been super good at sitting with all the other Black kids at the lunch table, which is to say I have struggled to feel welcome. It is not lost on me that even in another country, among a group of Black American artists from all over the United States, while slurping Japanese miso ramen in a major train station enveloped by Dutch-speaking voices, I could feel distant from my people, too.

The seat of Blackness is not located in the United States. Blackness, by its inherent revolutionary definition, is not ownable. It is by design, and deliberate, that we are estranged—abandoned by our country and then, again, ourselves. It is by design, and essential to the economics of our country and others, that our status here has always been ambiguous and endangered, and that we are inherently unable to return anywhere. This experience of placelessness, of violent hyphenation, is a condition we must vigilantly and creatively confront if we are to be made whole and healed, if we are to reclaim the trajectory of the boat, and return, finally, to ourselves. To each other. There are no chosen lands or chosen people. There are just Black people, being alive.

EVERYTHING IS (STILL) A SLAVE SHIP

For example, Jay-Z's music video for "Big Pimpin'" (dir. Hype Williams, 2000) starts on arrestingly blue water, follows the sun-dappled and seemingly endless ocean to a bright white boat full of Black people. The women silently gyrate, symbols for women; Jay-Z holds expensive jewelry to the camera lens, unleashes a flurry of green bills over a crowd of vibrantly costumed brown skin.

Tupac said, *We ain't even really rappin', we just letting our dead homies tell stories for us.*

When I look at Jay-Z backed by anonymous sexual female bodies I don't want to see the memory of rape on the slave ship but I do. When I see the gold bling around a Black man's neck I don't want to think about how many bodies were sold, but I do. I see signifiers for all the ways American capitalism uses and abuses Black labor and creativity.

When I see a chain I don't want to think of chains. When I see a boat I don't want to think about the boat that brought us. When I see the yacht I see the slave ship undone, in reverse. I don't want the slave ship to flicker in my memory, but it always does. As if this boat simply replaces that one—the yacht parked in the slave ship's spot. As if we haven't moved, we still haven't arrived, and I always remember how before, we were the merchandise, the dream of sex, the wad of cash.

"I'M NOTORIOUSLY TIGHT WITH VIDEO BUDGETS, BUT FOR 'BIG Pimpin',' I put out a million dollars," Jay wrote in his memoir *Decoded*. "We headed to Trinidad for Carnival, then booked a mansion in Miami, got the biggest yacht we could find, and hired hundreds of girls from the top agencies."

Hundreds of girls. I lose count of how many are doused with liquor. In a final frame, Dame even pours it on the camera, as if that's how little he gives a shit.

The Miami part was just for Pimp C, who had objected to flying to Trinidad, promised no more than eight bars, and upon arriving, refused to remove his mink coat for the shoot in ninety-plus weather. "TV ain't got no temperature," he'd reportedly explained to Jigga.

Pimp C performs his verse shirtless except for a shiny gold pendant and the mink, a light-skinned woman in her own white mink coat grinding vacantly against his tattooed belly. Her cowgirl-inspired getup is all white and complete with a fringed bikini and white mink wide-brimmed hat, obscuring her eyes as she mouths the chorus. At some point near the end of his verse, the camera's lowered perspective moves even lower, the swaying crotch of her white pants filling the entire frame. The subservient camera angles employed throughout the video indulge at least two male fantasies simultaneously: allowing the rappers to talk down to the viewer and dangle their oversized chains atop our heads, as if to inspire submission to the bigness of their pimpin' and also allowing access to shamelessly bountiful crotch shots.

> *If I wasn't rappin', baby*
> *I would still be ridin' Mercedes*
> *Coming down and sippin' daily*
> *No record til whitey pay me*

Eight bars was enough to make Pimp C's lines some of the song's most enduringly memorable, his Texas twang its own music—part of it would show up as the first lines of Kendrick Lamar's 2011 "Blow My High (Members Only)," its tonal rhythm (*smokin' out/pourin' up*) the song's guiding pentameter, *R.I.P. Aaliyah* its final refrain.

IN THE WEEKS LEADING UP TO THE VIDEO SHOOT, JAY-Z WAS EM-broiled in a lawsuit for assaulting the guy who leaked the album—his fourth—a month before its official release date; he found himself examining the rage that seemed to overtake him in the moment, made him lose all sense of cool, made him forget where and who he was. "The streets can start to make you see the logic in violence," he wrote in his memoir. "If a thing surrounds you and is targeted at you, it can start to seem regular."

After finally turning himself in at a Midtown New York precinct, Shawn Carter realized how serious it was, "because they started setting up a press conference. The district attorney had his publicist on the phone, the cop that was assigned to do the perp walk with me was combing his hair and fixing his collar; it was a complete show for them. The hilarious thing, if any of this can be considered funny, is that the Rocawear bubble coat I was wearing when they paraded me in front of the cameras started flying off the shelves the last three weeks before Christmas."

When I see record sales and record company execs, products and paparazzi, consumption of Black soul and skin as entertainment, buyable and sellable, I wish I didn't see us getting bought and sold over and over, auctioned, exploited, haggled over, put to work, put on display, the same old illusions of agency and ownership dressed up in new contractual terms and scalped minks.

I wish I didn't see it because I feel it.

. . .

Pimp (noun): Trader of flesh for profit. Controller of labor
    and law. Protector. Abuser. Employer. Enforcer.
Pimp (verb): To flaunt or adorn.

BY 2000, HIP-HOP WAS FIRMLY IN THE HANDS AND HEARTS OF
whites. Eminem was no Vanilla Ice, more than just fly for a
white guy, and certain kinds of white people jumped at the
long-desired excuse to say the N-word ("It's part of the song!").
'Twas the age of "wiggas" and "acting white" and my sixth-
grade classmates, Black and white, calling me an Oreo—the
white classmates often suggesting they were "blacker than me"
("on the inside"). 'Twas the age of JNCO jeans and FUBU and
liking Tupac being indicators of Blackness. 'Twas the age of
white people feeling comfortable—supported, even—saying
such things. By then, though, white was white and "gangsta
rap" was not, and whether or not the president played the
saxophone (he didn't), he was still a white guy with a southern-
bent accent who got off on drug charges for which hustlers
like Jay-Z, by then, were serving decades of time—as an
"example"—and ballooning private prisons for political gain.

Released just in time to be the summer anthem, "Big
Pimpin'" was HOV's biggest single to date, and its excessive
video laid the red carpet for early 2000s indulgence and
canonized what came to be the rappers-on-yachts cliché,
which only solidifies its relevancy in American pop culture
and, probably, its impact on how white Americans view Black
artists and regard Black success.

It had been decided that the song, the final single on the album, would be not only a hit, but also a game changer. Jay describes the ambitious excitement as he "rallied the troops" after hearing Timbaland's beat. "I told my staff to get us on MTV's *Making the Video*, which hadn't been on a rap set before." "Big Pimpin'" was to commemorate the ushering of a new sound and swag—indeed, a new millennium of Black music, Black masculinity, and Blacks on boats. It would invite and underscore a new image and era of both Black wealth and Black worth.

"The contrast between the million-dollar extravagance of the "Big Pimpin'" video and the potential of being behind bars for years [over] a mindless assault was not lost on me," HOV wrote. "Both were about losing control."

Maybe, when there's so little over which you have control, it's within your right to lose it.

"If the price is life, you better get what you paid for."

THE FIRST FOUR NOTES OF "BIG PIMPIN'" ARE NOW INEXTRICA-ble from *let's ri/i/i/i/i/ide*, its flute's cadence now timed to ocean's ripples and boobie jiggles. "Timbaland went wild on that track; he used pieces of North African music, horns that sounded damn near like geese." There is a sample at the heart of the song's composition, but its origins became irrelevant, erased, under new ownership: A song can be a slave ship, too.

The pieces in question, four highly recognizable and virtually undisguised notes of Egyptian composer Baligh Hamdi's "Khosara Khosara"—("What a loss, what a loss")—resulted in a suit against Jay-Z and Timbaland and Linkin Park (who sampled the sample on a mash-up album that defined my middle school years) and a legal battle that would last almost ten years. Osama Fahmy, a relative of the composer, filed the lawsuit claiming that Timbaland's use of said North African music infringed on copyright terms and violated Hamdi's "moral rights" according to Egyptian law. "They used it with a song that, even by Jay-Z's own admission, is very vulgar and base," Fahmy's lawyer told *The Guardian*. "They not only took music without paying. They're using it in a song that is, frankly, disgusting."

In court, Jay testified, "I didn't think there was a sample in it." His job, he said, was to make music. Producer Timbaland, in an effort to argue and illustrate the relative inconsequence of the sample's four notes in the making of the song (and following the malfunction of his prop keyboard), beatboxed. Lest there be any confusion as to who can use who, the California judge ruled on the basis of legality over morality, in favor of US law and Jay-Z et al.

IT'S IMPORTANT TO NOTE THE DIFFERENT CONNOTATIONS AND consequences of *pimpin* (adjective), *pimpin'* (verb) or *to pimp* (verb) (e.g., *Pimp My Ride* featuring Xzibit) as opposed to *pimp* (noun) or *to pimp* (verb) as in "to pimp out." Wherein the direct object of the active verb of *pimping* is in all likelihood a woman's body.

In the decades that followed its release, HOV and his crew publicly discussed their changing feelings about the song lyrics and especially the video. Roc-A-Fella Records co-founder Damon "Dame" Dash—Champagne Dame, back then, but fourteen years later, a father—apologized "to all the girls I poured champagne [on]" and admitted to embarrassment over his twentysomething foolishness. He said in an interview with Hip Hop Motivation, "I don't even know that guy."

The song's message, he realized only after recognizing how it might impact, and what it might be communicating to, both his daughter and his son, had been misguided and foolish.

Rap, we all know is a young man's game. Foolishness is almost necessary. The game is one of comeuppance, an extension of the dozens or the Soul Train line or both. Maybe all rap is battle rap. Maybe "Big Pimpin'" is exactly what it sounds like—inherently violent and exploitative, dependent first and foremost upon women's disposability and abuse.

You know I thug 'em, fuck 'em, love 'em, leave 'em
Cause I don't fuckin' need 'em

In a 2010 interview, Jay-Z lamented of the song: "I can't believe I said that. And kept saying it. What kind of animal would say this sort of thing?"

IN 2009, "RAP COMEDY TRIO" AND *SATURDAY NIGHT LIVE* ALUMS The Lonely Island released a spoof of the rappers-on-yachts "cliché," and specifically the then-iconic (or cliché) "Big Pimpin'" video, called "I'm on a Boat." It features the troupe of young white men joined by autotune prince T-Pain spitting goofy, simplistic bars aboard an extravagant yacht, stuff like, "*Everybody look at me / 'cause I'm sailing on a boat.*" Their singles before and after, also produced by *SNL* shorts, were called, respectively, "Jizz in My Pants" and "I Just Had Sex." I mean, they were funny. We watched in our college dorms—by then rappers on boats were fodder for mockery, not praise or admiration or even begrudging respect.

Andy Samberg retains that indie-darling-goofball charm, and *SNL*-vetted material is just that—network approved for white audiences whether or not they've met a Black person in real life. It's all in good fun! (Ain't it always?)

In the video, and in subsequent live performances, including one backed by hip-hop icons the Roots, Samberg and the rest of the Lonely Island don tuxes and crew attire, top hats and captain hats, respectively. In his, Jay-Z dons an era-appropriate bucket hat. Both videos feature the distinct camera angle that emphasizes hierarchy—hands flapping in the camera's low-positioned frame—and women's crotches.

Crotches, asses, crotches, cash, ass, ass, celebration.

There is nothing alarming or historically transgressive about white men on a yacht flaunting wealth and power. Nor is there anything new about white men "spoofing" Black success, dismissing chunks of Black culture as ridiculous and juvenile, like bumbling children playing dress up in rented costume jewelry—simultaneously iconizing and belittling Black men in one gesture. "*Never thought I'd be on a boat,*" the song goes.

It went platinum.

Defying the inherent laws of spoof, "I'm on a Boat" was

even nominated for a Best Rap/Sung Collaboration Grammy. Still, lest there be any confusion as to who reigns where and has the reins to what, it was none other than Jay-Z, Kanye, and Rihanna who won the category for their song, "Run This Town." (*"We running this, let's go,"* Andy Samberg says to the other white guy at the end of the first verse.)

"Never thought I'd see the day / When a big boat coming my way," T-Pain croons in a top hat, virtually daring us not to call it minstrelsy, not to see the dark irony.

Niggas on yachts cannot be serious, they're saying.

Vol. 3 . . . Life and Times of S. Carter had gone triple platinum.

"Everyone seems to think that the Negro is easily imitated when nothing could be further from the truth," Zora Neale Hurston wrote in 1934, at the peak of what she calls a "baffling" trend of black-faced white performers ("good comedians, but damn poor niggers") whose attempts "are misplaced or distorted by the accent falling on the wrong element." Distorted through caricature and misarticulation, warped by white expectations, by a deep misunderstanding and disregard for our cultural contributions if unable to capitalize on them.

"The Negro's universal mimicry is . . . evidence of something that permeates [their] entire self. And that thing is drama." Every part of our lives, "no matter how joyful or how sad," she says, "is highly dramatized." In every moment we find "sufficient poise for drama. Everything is acted out." Sex acts, swagger, ship-captaining, spending, pimping: "little plays by strolling players" performed daily.

"Who has not observed a robust young Negro chap posing upon a street corner possessed of nothing but his clothing, his strength and his youth?"

Rappers on boats: What little power we have in their
world, we flaunt and flex. We talk down to your gaze. We
revel in being an imposition.

Hurston's "Characteristics of Negro Expression" lists a
dozen other modes of self-assertion and markers of Black
creative culture, among them folklore, dancing (and relat-
edly, "angularity"), "absence of the concept of privacy" (being
up in one another's business), originality (or "the modifica-
tion of ideas"), the Jook (da club), and, second only to drama,
the "will to adorn." Even where it disturbs and disregards
"conventional standards," ornament "satisfies the soul of this
creator. In this respect the American Negro has done wonders for the English language," contributing "1) the use of
simile and metaphor; 2) the use of the double descriptive;
3) the use of verbal nouns (and making nouns from verbs)."
Our speech, clothing, and even home decor reflect "the urge
to adorn," giving the sense that "there can never be enough
of beauty, let alone too much."

Citing the lush languid sermons of religious services and
the Negro prayer's poetic superiority to even the Old Testament, she writes, "Whatever the Negro does of his own volition he embellishes." What is unsaid: how often our very
states of being and behaving is not of our own volition, how
starved for our selfhood we were before.

I have a cultural memory and a long one. My whole body
remembers the boat—the violence of its transformation of

person into capital, from flesh into function. When I see capitalism, and Black creativity, and sexually exploited Black women, and Black bodies on display or otherwise for sale, on a boat above water, from which and into our souls were thrown, I see our story.

I see Black America: how it started the same way, on another boat, how it's always about money and a woman is only as good as the way golden sunlight reflects off her ass. A new narrative made up of the same elements as before and before and before. Transposed over Jay-Z's swag is the history and essence of all our bards and entertainers, our wordplay and braggadocio and fashion, our preachers and performance. I see Black America: rappers on boats. Storytellers and survivors in the middle of the ocean.

WEDDING SEASON (NOCTURNE FOR SANDRA BLAND)

I was excited when I RSVP'd. It would be a lovely way to end the tour, I thought, maybe even comforting— a balm for the months of nightly performances, all the new faces. I secretly love weddings despite the bitter hopelessness loudly knocking on the door to my temperamental heart. I get to dress up, there's tons of wine, the social atmosphere is easy because everybody at least wants to be in a good mood, and, aided by said wine, I'll be goddamned if witnessing the weight and depth of commitment and certainty of love doesn't make me cry a little bit, every time. Either because it's the stuff of Lisa Frank unicorns and Pixar fairy tales, or because (in spite of and in spite of and in spite of), I believe it for myself, for everybody. Maybe I'm a sucker.

The plan was to connect in Dallas from Arizona and land at LaGuardia (that would be the worst part), pick up a rental car at the airport, and have a *chill* drive to Hudson, New York, land of millennial weddings and trendy second homes, about two hours away.

But, as too many people had already hinted, the plan was far too ambitious—I'd started feeling sick two cities ago, and I was generally broken down, unraveling in airports. Whatever. I'd started taking mood stabilizers before my tour and was invigorated by the promise of such an extraordinary idea, a stabile mood.

I'm always excited when I RSVP.

Another problem with the plan is that it was 2017, which meant that for the past two years, anytime I drove alone at night, anytime I saw blue lights in the rearview, anytime I drove alone on a highway at the mercy of unfamiliar landscapes, and actually, every three days in between—brushing my teeth, or taking my meds, or seeing a bumper sticker about my life mattering, or seeing a commercial about mental health mattering, or if my mind wandered to any future beyond tomorrow—I thought of Sandra Bland.

On the Dallas flight I could not get water. Twice, I asked the Dolly Parton–blond flight attendant and after making eye contact, she legitimately looked away. After the third time, a young mom in the aisle seat had mercy enough to be a White Savior and go to the back to get me one of those little half bottles.

From Arizona to Dallas, my requests were ignored to my

face—my requests for the one inalienable requirement for being an alive person. I was too tired to feel slighted and invisible, again, in transit, helplessly gawking at the rampant preferential treatment around me, the data and disappointment. And when I was on the ground, what I did every day was perform. I cried in the Dallas terminal bathroom after a white woman bumped me as she passed and didn't apologize.

LaGuardia was LaGuardia—I heard someone once describe it, perfectly and hilariously, as akin to a hallway. My plane is hours late and I arrive at the rental car place at almost midnight, tired enough to get a bottle of Coke from the vending machine, and there's a whole drama in there—a full and properly inconvenient breakdown, everything covered from fear of lifelong loneliness and aloneness, the heaviness of expectation, the self-punishment, never admitting I'm tired, punking out. I had created the mess I was in, and worse, I had created the kind of life that could reap this kind of mess. I even called my parents for an extra serving of I-told-you-so.

When I finally get my rental car, which is decades younger than mine and too "smart" for me, I seem to circle the same two blocks of Queens in the pitch-dark before pulling over and crying again. It's pitiful. I hate myself for it. I can't get the Bluetooth thing to work, I get obsessed with trying to make the Bluetooth thing work, I don't know where I'm going, I don't think my lights are on, this car is not on my side. I wonder if I should or can or will fold on the wedding.

I realistically do not know how to use this car, it is the middle of the night, how shitty is it to cancel right before a wedding? They'd probably already ordered my food, right?

I don't want to fail just because I'm alone. I say a bunch of mean things to myself until I decide to go back to the plan.

Finally on the dark road heading upstate from Queens, empty but for a few semi trucks, I was scared, hesitating even as I sped up. The whole day was bullying me to give up. Into giving up on myself. I didn't want to prove myself right.

It was starting to look like wilderness, which is to say I started to think about Sandra Bland. As I drove I worried: If I were to slip up handling the unfamiliar vehicle and its screens and buttons. If I started frantically and idiotically crying again. If I got tired and drove too slow. If I tried to keep up with other cars and went too fast. If I were to pull over. If I were to *be* pulled over. If the cop happened to be a white man from the wilderness. No witnesses, one subtle movement in the deep dark, and just what am I doing out here driving this road at this time of night? Why was I alone, where was I going, why are my eyes so red? If they claimed I killed myself, it would be believable, everyone knows I have suicidal thoughts.

Anything could happen. Anybody could say anything happened.

After her death in 2015, Sandra Bland visited my thoughts daily; now I'm down to just once a week. I google her name, irrationally hoping the cause of death will have a different word after its colon. It's not just that she was around my age, it's how the death ruling is so effective and final. It's her smile, and how the word *suicide* shut her up for good. How she was starting a new job the next week. How she acknowledged her mental illness. The video she posted, eloquent and passionate and proudly Black, condemning police brutality. She was pulled over for a broken taillight (ain't it always that?), and after that, "hanged herself" in a cell at the empty jail.

I already knew the stakes of Driving While Black, how they fluctuated county line to county line (that part we'd known since Till), how important it was to be faultless, and how that probably wouldn't matter in the end. When I see someone's on my tail and I'm already doing close to eighty, I just think, that person must not be Black.

Risk. Our particularly heightened sense of doom produces in us a skill for continually and quickly evaluating risk. An additional region of the brain is devoted to this analysis, gathering sensory information in order to be one step ahead. Two or three if you can make it. Otherwise, hide. You never know what they can get away with in the dark.

Every Black person has a victim who hits hardest. Whose death at the hands of the police changes everything—about how and how often you step off the front porch, how you interpret every gaze at the grocery store, whether or not and whom you date, the list of ambitions you hope to accomplish before it's your turn.

. . .

BACK AT THE RENTAL CAR OFFICE, I ADMIT MY DEFEAT AND RE-
turn the keys. That night, instead of staying with friends, I
sleep at a hotel in Flushing that's also an all-night karaoke
bar.

I'm what you call a "high-functioning" depressive. Which
is a fancy way of saying I can "pass" as someone not having a
nervous breakdown, even when I am, that my depressive episodes seem, for other people, to come "out of nowhere." Being
a Black woman is another way to say I can "pass" for someone
unneeding and undeserving of help. A high-functioning single
Black woman: redundantly no one's concern.

The next morning it's back to the suitcases, all the effort,
no witnesses.

NATIONAL EMERGENCIES

*Like desire, language disrupts, refuses to be
contained within boundaries. –bell hooks*

February 2019 in Washington, DC. I'm "just one" on
a barstool in the restaurant of a hotel that is not my own,
waiting out a downpour. An obnoxious couple nearby touches
knees, their flirtatious laughter filling space like church perfume.

I've been assigned to write about one of the landmark
court cases in the ACLU's triumphant one-hundred-year
past. Though I'd never heard of it before, I chose my case,
Bob Jones University v. United States, because the description
crosses multiple categories where I have particular insight.
Familiar phrases leaped out like an autobiographical bingo
sheet: Christian school, interracial relationships, discrimina-
tion, beliefs. My research into the school has led me to a
sermon by the university's founder, Pastor Bob Jones Sr., de-

livered Easter Sunday 1960 over the university radio air-waves, to be subsequently published for sale at the university bookstore, under the title "Is Segregation Scriptural?"

The title of the sermon is not really a question, yet there a question mark dangles, taking the joke too far.

I've been assigned to write about my life, and my life has led me here, to these familiar words, lamenting the view, an outsider. It is very clear to me what I am allowed to expect and want from my American life, and too easily, I follow the rules. Maybe because I hate myself, but maybe because I know I am hated, how long I have been, and in how many ways.

It's the day after Valentine's Day, and the president has declared a national emergency *Concerning the Southern Border of the United States*. I'm not especially lonely, but I am alone, and I'm beginning to understand why part of me believes I deserve to be.

AS MOST AMERICANS ARE CERTAINLY FAMILIAR, ANYONE CAN use the Bible to prove anything. Much like a poem—or, for instance, the Constitution—interpretation may be subjective. Its authors are consistently debated, and either way, long gone, so the text is fair game. Rather than seeking the text's intention, analyzing it in its historical context (as one might in a course on theology, law, or literature), many preachers (or, say, Supreme Court judges)—whom, it should be noted, are often not scholars but self-appointed messengers—approach the text with their personal convictions about what constitutes faithfulness, what constitutes right.

At its most beautiful, language is the secret weapon for understanding how we relate, how we make sense of the terms of our weird world. Or it can be another kind of weapon, sharpened in the hands of the stubborn or the extremist. Words are ductile, delicate, and loaded like that. We entrust our spiritual leaders with our hearts. We're seduced by their words like a politician's or a slick-talking attorney's, their rhetoric of *War On* ____ and *officer-involved*, their definitions of *person* and *thing*. Any word can be a code word.

As a product of white evangelical education, I instantly know the words to Bob Jones's arguments. In fact, the Statement of Faith and Position Statement currently posted on the website for the K-to-12 Bob Jones Academy are practically identical to those posted by the two Christian schools I attended from pre-kindergarten through twelfth grade. It's the same rhetoric I encountered in chapels and classrooms where I sat befuddled, terrified, and ashamed, as youth group leaders or pale Bible teachers presented rigorously fabricated interpretations of Scripture. There are some slick acrobatics involved in manipulating text as a secondary source to prove the claims of a primary source. To spin your own opinion into a priori truth, mince and manipulate language and listeners until yours are the only words.

This impassioned genre of debate, this art of war, is well suited for fundamentalist, evangelical white Christians, Ivy League dinner parties, and people like me, who are bullheaded. Therefore, I'm calling bullshit on Bob Jones's whole platform.

THE WHITE CHRISTIANS OF MY CHILDHOOD WERE DEALERS OF instruction and discipline, and they shaped my early understandings of correctness and human history. Of the world outside the small, sun-filled school. I wanted to please my teachers, I wanted to be good, and their place at the front of the class was a blinding light in my line of vision.

One of the first doctrines I absorbed from my zealous teachers-slash-missionaries was that the world was split between those inside, and those outside—a truth made unwaveringly clear as landscapes and demographics transformed on the drive from school to my house. Our side of town felt darker, less pure; my family's values not stringent or steadfast enough. However I squinted or covered my eyes, we'd never resemble the royal family from *7th Heaven*, looking like a stock photo in a frame etched with the word *Blessings*.

I feared for us and pitied us—was it even possible for us to see the world washed in so much warm light, to be protected from our own darkness? Was it because we were African Americans, was it because of that damned silent hyphen between us and every *them*?

Things were either Christian or secular, "of the world." "Secular": the way my elementary school teachers' faces contorted angrily as they railed against Harry Potter, or skirts above the calf, or *South Park*, or N*Sync. The judgmental way my friends offered to pray for me and my ongoing struggle to resist the dangerous allure of worldly things, almost as if my urges were more intense than theirs—what was it about how I looked or acted that made them assume I needed to be saved, by them, in their way?

Maybe that's part of how I became "not really Black, though." Because I was among them, defying their believed profile of Black Americans, which was mostly from *Cops*. Mostly secular.

What I learned was fear. Every interpretation of Scripture was a warning. In every Bible class lesson, every youth pastor's message, and every memorized Bible verse, I heard "or else." The line between good and bad was clear. You are in, or else you are out. This is how I learned the ecosystems of trespass and punishment.

DO NOT LET ANYTHING DISTURB YOU, BOB JONES COMMANDS AT the start of the sermon. A theme is established. It hangs in the air throughout his address, in the bedrooms of each supposition. It always comes back to this language.

Disturbance, protection. Vigilance. Unrest, purity.

"Is Segregation Scriptural?" includes very little Scripture. The whole sermon hinges on a single word, in a single verse, in a single chapter in the Book of Acts—Acts 17:26:

And [God] hath made of one blood all nations of men for to dwell on all faces of the earth, and hath determined the times before appointed, and the bounds of their habitation.

"That says that God Almighty fixed the bounds of their habitation," the pastor reiterates, blasphemously disregarding the rest of the verse and neglecting to analyze the passages surrounding it.

"God never meant to have one race," he misinterprets assuredly. "God never meant for America to be a melting pot to rub out the line between the nations. That was not God's purpose . . ."

Even on Easter, the day of the Resurrection, a story of transformation and renewal, the ultimate lesson of sacrifice, he preaches with unforgiving anger, from a spirit he might call passion, but I call panic. I am a woman, so people are always reminding me to leave my emotions out of things, but no one has reminded Bob that emotions compromise your chances of ever being taken seriously.

"I say it makes me sick!" he bellows, as if our very presence, our sheer proximity, scourges him with the physical force of a tumor or contagion. How dramatic—as if getting too close to us is a hazard to a white Christian body.

The boundaries of our habitation include: countries of origin (which he recklessly conflates with race), restaurants, public pools, train cars and buses, and, of course, wedding chapels and sexual relations. Build a wall around all these things, all these different kinds of bodies, and we "will have no trouble."

ON THE TV ABOVE THE BAR, THE PRESIDENT HOLDS A PRESS conference in the White House Rose Garden. He is demanding billions of dollars to build fifty-five miles of heavily patrolled, barbed fencing along the border of Mexico and the United States—a country ostensibly founded by immigrants who trespassed their bounds of habitation and invaded the borders of this land, consumed its resources, and violently displaced its people. The president welcomes some tearful mothers whose children were killed by undocumented people; one young son was killed when his motorcycle crashed into a car being driven by an undocumented immigrant.

"We are talking about an invasion," the president says. "An invasion of drugs, invasion of gangs, invasion of people and it's unacceptable."

Last year, the president shut down the government altogether, an anti-immigration standoff with Congress to block the DREAM Act and extort funding for the US-Mexico border wall he'd campaigned on—1,000 miles of steel. *What is it about the wall,* I kept thinking, *why does he need the physical structure?*

That just ended two weeks ago. It was the longest shutdown in United States history.

"I didn't have to do this," the president snarks.

National emergency sounds like imminent danger, like an actual emergency. National emergency sounds like war.

BOB JONES UNIVERSITY WASN'T ONE OF THE CHRISTIAN COLleges represented on our high school's graduating class map. Bob Jones Sr. is not a famous evangelist like Jerry Falwell,

Billy Graham, or James Dobson—any one of those pastors from Christian radio commercials or whose sermons my middle school Bible teachers assigned for extra credit. He's just one in a bumbling, bellowing chorus spewing centuries-old heresy.

Still, I've been carrying a beat-up printout of the pamphlet from city to city, reading the question "Is Segregation Scriptural?" every day with new comprehension and sharpening bitterness, seething as I trace the lineage of his words to the teachings of my youth—the internalized belief that where I belong is on the outside, that loneliness is what I get.

I'm not shocked by the racism of a white pastor in 1960 South Carolina, the biblical defense of segregation and specifically anti-miscegenation, the whitewashing of the effects of slavery, or the need to make God say what you say. I know there is no use in debating these men. But I know it's foolish to ignore them.

I have a habit of paying too much attention to language— which words are used when, and with what intonation, and what other words might be underneath them, unspoken, unconscious, or fantasized. Words pinch me without warning, their endless definitions unfurling in my psyche. Words like *Only one?* or *Mind a seat at the end of the bar?*

Actually, it's not a habit. It's a learned response.

I WISH I COULD PUT THIS SERMON OUT OF MY MIND, THROW away its pages. What I want to do is write my essay about Bob Jones Sr. and racist white Christians and being conditioned to feel undesirable and all that, toss away this thick pamphlet of trash, walk away unemotionally, unaffected.

But now that I've read it, I keep hearing it, and I know I'll always hear it. And I'll understand someone thinks it, that its words are somewhere inside America, and that as an American, its words are inside me, too. I know beliefs like this are what made me, what got me here.

Tonight in February 2019, we have a crisis of language. People are calling other people aliens. According to the president's proclamation, "the current situation" poses a "humanitarian crisis that threatens core national security interests." And the emergency is the way they say *threaten*, and what they mean when they use the word *protection*; how definitions dissolve on their tongues, how easily they call themselves God, how often that becomes the truth.

Once again seated like an afterthought at a bar top near a bustling kitchen, I decide I will no longer respond to restaurant hosts with "Yeah, just me" like it's a consolation. Like I'm not enough.

By definition, a border is not a wall.

THEY HAD THE RIGHT IDEA, BOB SAYS, WITH SEGREGATION. IT was actually a tidy and ultimately positive outcome to the unfortunate but forgiven sin of chattel slavery in the United States.

He says, "That was wrong. But God overruled. When they came over here"—(and I could spend paragraphs on the usage of this word *came*, not to mention the fixation on victims, they, rather than perpetrators)—"many of them did not know the Bible and did not know about Jesus Christ; but they got converted. Some of the greatest preachers the world has ever known were colored preachers who were converted in slavery days . . . God Almighty allowed these colored people to be turned here into the South and over-ruled what happened and then he turned the colored people into wonderful Christian people."

The slave trade had been, essentially, an extended missionary trip.

"Did you colored people ever stop to think where you might have been if that had not happened?"

That piercingly functionless question mark. The passive *happened*, stripped of its action and agent.

"Now, you colored people listen to me . . . You might be over there in jungles of Africa today, unsaved."

According to Bob, after God adjusted his unflinching and crystal clear will and "permitted the slaves to come over to America," it was us African Americans who didn't follow God's will—a baseless accusation that our purpose in being (no, coming) here was "so that the colored people could be the great missionaries to the Africans." Instead, we settled in. We crossed the borders of our assigned plantations and started having sex with the good white people, trampling divine order.

"The white people in America would have helped pay their way over there. By the hundred and hundred they could have gone back to Africa and got the Africans converted after the slavery days were over." This is news to me! In all my years of hearing "go back to Africa," I never knew there were checks being waved around.

Besides, *could* and *would* are theoretical assumptions, which are their own violent privilege. They remove the inescapability of reality, of what is and isn't so. Good white Christians can live in service of what is unseen with easy disregard for the world they inhabit.

I'm constantly implored to look past what is evident. To imagine having a viewpoint that ignores my lived experiences. To forgive whenever I'm excluded. I'm always being reminded of good white people, being asked to state for the record that I don't hate all white people. Here, the schism of thought between us and them. They are personalized where we are theoretical. They, as individuals, can be singled out as exceptions, they can be one of the good ones. They can be excused from any guilt or responsibility for African American plight if they themselves did not own slaves—and we are haunted by the reality that our American consciousness stems from inequality, insufficiency. There are those who have—who have always been able to have—and those whose lives are consolations. This is about power. Who gets to call who an emergency.

The fear—buried as it is in absurd flights of revisionist accounts of past and present race relations in the South—is specific and pointed. The problem is the mixing. The problem is all of this progress, this change.

If we separate ourselves, draw up borders and differentiations, we can more easily profit off one another without guilt. If budging is against our religion, it's easy to condemn immigration and integration; the disappearing lines of habitation; the sense of being invaded.

Is not integration—including cohabitation, interracial sex, equal voting rights, and blended education—a consequence, a natural and inevitable outcome of the finances and practices of slavery? In every account I've heard, it was the slave owner who got in bed with the slave.

PENNED BY THEOLOGIAN GEORGE ARMSTRONG AND PUBLISHED by Charles Scribner in 1857, *The Christian Doctrine of Slavery* comprises six chapters describing slavery as an "incidental evil" rather than a sin; arguing that Christ and his Apostles saw fit to list sins and offenses in a "numerous, and some instances, extended and minute manner," yet "slaveholding does not appear in any catalogue of sins or disciplinable offenses." Armstrong's conclusion states that according to Scripture, the Church is instructed only to "labor to make 'good masters and good slaves.'"

Pastor Armstrong reasons that "God has assigned to the church and the state each its own separate province, and neither has ever intruded into the province of the other without suffering therefor. To the church God has entrusted all the interests of man which more immediately concern the life to come," whereas the state is in charge of interests concerning "this present life—all questions of respecting capital and labor, civil rights and political franchises, the protection of the weak, the forcible repression of crime, and the general administration of justice between man and man."

Imagine claiming Christianity, and seriously arguing that none of the above is of your concern, technically. That protecting the weak and advocating justice are simply not in your jurisdiction. Imagine being a spiritual leader, an American citizen, for whom it is possible to be concerned with only the life to come.

"The African Slave, in our Southern United States may be deeply degraded; the debasing effects of generations of sin may, at first sight, seem to have almost obliterated his humanity," but even "the slave race" should hear the Gospel. Like it or not, he seems to wink with his italics, the Bible says to "'go ye into *all the world* and preach the Gospel to *every creature.*'"

"With the ultimate effect of this upon the civil and political position of the slave the Church has nothing directly to do."

This remained the prevailing general sentiment of white Christian leaders until and throughout the civil rights movement; one hundred and three years later the same wrong words find themselves spilling out of Bob Jones's big mouth.

In 1960, mere months before Bob Jones Sr. insisted on the radio that "no two races ever lived as close together as the white people and colored people in the South and got along so well," four Negro college students refused to leave the lunch counter of a Woolworths and were met by spit in their faces, cigarettes burned into their skin. This was in Greensboro, North Carolina, 189 miles from Bob Jones's

Greenville, South Carolina—where just one year earlier Jackie Robinson had been asked by airport police to vacate a white-only waiting area.

In 1954, the year Ruby Bridges was born, *Brown v. Board of Education* ruled the segregation of public schools unconstitutional, prompting such white backlash as a southern sheriff's doubling down on "states' rights," lawmakers sharpening their tongues on words like *tradition*, and Reverend Carey Daniel at First Baptist Church of West Dallas proclaiming God "the original segregationist." In Jackson, Mississippi, an address entitled "A Christian View on Segregation" was delivered and published by the retiring president of Belhaven University.

The New Orleans judge who'd ordered the first day of public school integration statewide, finally granting Ruby her birthright in spite of the boycotting parents and prevailing southern "tradition," was soon politically and socially ostracized; he and his family would vacate their hometown within two years.

In 1960, four US Marshals were deployed to Louisiana to escort six-year-old Ruby Bridges to her freshly integrated public school, after the child and her family began receiving death threats. Every day, all year, federal agents walked Ruby to and from school, where all year, she would sit in a classroom of one.

"This disturbing movement is not of God," Bob Jones preached about civil rights. "It is Satanic."

That summer, Greenville's segregated public library

would be the site of a protest sit-in by the Greenville Eight, among them college freshman Jesse Jackson, whose pastor posted their bail.

One year later, in 1961, Air Force vet and model Jackson State student James Meredith applied for admission at the University of Mississippi and was twice denied. Aided by Medgar Evers and the NAACP Legal Defense Fund, he then brought suit to the US district of a state whose Democratic leader had pledged, "no school will be integrated in Mississippi while I am your governor," with the ultimate goal of pressuring the Kennedy administration to enforce the Brown ruling. Following months of petty firewalls and blockages, including new and abridged state laws, convictions against Meredith, and vetoes against admissions officials, Governor Barnett of Mississippi was found in contempt and given an ultimatum with a price tag of $10,000 for every day he refused to soften.

Barnett went back and forth on the phone with US Attorney General Robert F. Kennedy, until relenting, and made a watery pledge to ensure civil peace. This time, the armed forces dispatched for Meredith's first day of classes included hundreds of US Marshals, US Border Patrol agents, and Federal Bureau of Prisons officers; but the night before, after local whites descended on the campus and ignited what would come to be known as the Ole Miss riot of 1962, the Kennedy administration sent in the Mississippi National Guard, too. The next morning, as federal agents patched wounds from thrown rocks, car skeletons dripped ashes, the city surveyed expensive damages, and two families grieved in shock, James Meredith became the first Black student enrolled at the University of Mississippi.

By 1965, when the Voting Rights Act passed, even though all the public colleges in South Carolina had been desegregated, Bob Jones U remained a stanch holdout. In 1966, thirty-two-year-old Meredith, who would earn a law degree from Columbia in a few years' time, embarked alone on a 220-mile March Against Fear from Memphis to Jackson, Tennessee, encouraging voter registration, and despite governor-pledged police protection, he took bullets to the back and legs from a local white gunman who pled guilty without explanation.

In 1967, *Loving v. Virginia* legalized interracial marriage in the United States. Bob Jones University only began to admit Black students four years later, in 1971—provided they were married, and to another Black person. Meanwhile, in 1970, the Internal Revenue Service had amended previous regulations to specify that only private schools without discriminatory admissions policies would be allowed to claim a tax exemption status. Bob Jones University ignored this, opting instead to file a suit petitioning the school's revoked exemption status, on the basis of the First Amendment. In 1975, still involved in a drawn-out legal battle with the courts, still illegally receiving tax cuts and determined to make the case for their entitlement to such privileges, the university conceded to allow admission to single Black students—provided they were not engaged in, or known to advocate for, interracial unions.

No wonder that in 1990, my place in my white evangelical preschool felt like a favor. Why I didn't feel I belonged in the churchgoing, Sarah Palin–voting households of my friends from school, like I would ever model their Christian values. Why I felt that because of my color, I could never be fully saved, unless given a pass for my Blackness, which, in scriptural language, carried with it corruption, imperfection. Sin. And the wages of sin is death. It's one of the first things they teach us.

By the late seventies and the establishment of the "Association of Christian Schools International" (known to us as ACSI)—which accredited my schools, too—Bob Jones University had begun publishing "Christ-centered" classroom and homeschool curriculum through Bob Jones University Press.

Once a modest textbook distributor, BJU Press exploded in popularity and production scale during the early nineties boom of homeschooling and privately accredited Christian schools, aided by conservative parents still high off the already-debunked myth of rampant suburban Satanism, early fanatical whisperings of Y2K apocalypse, and the overwhelming interfaith Christian disapproval of *Roe v. Wade*. With politics gaining importance with religious leaders, and religion squarely in politics, there was more demand for non-secular, "faith-based" curricula. By the time I started preschool, and throughout the nineties, BJU Press was one of the largest US publishers of K through 12 educational materials with a "Christian worldview," including the 1997 text, *Free Indeed: Heroes of Black Christian History*.

Bob Jones could have taught me the alphabet, US history, penmanship, creationism, arithmetic, or whatever else, were it not that the administrators at my school preferred the materials of rival publisher A Beka Book.

That's the thing, though. Maybe I was fed Bob Jones curriculum: an errant handout here or there, a set of flashcards, or sing-along cassettes. It was all ACSI-accredited.

BJU retained tax exempt status until 1983, when the ACLU intervened and the Supreme Court ruled against the university's First Amendment argument. But by then, their beliefs were already seeded. Besides, interracial marriages and romantic relationships were still prohibited under the university's code of conduct—and continued to be until 2000, after coming to public light when the school was visited by none other than the adolescent president of my adolescence, George W. Bush.

My white high school boyfriend—who lasted for such a short time and the relationship ended with such disdain that I do not even count him in my list of boyfriends (thereby clearing the list)—was quickly sat down by his dry, devout father after I entered the picture and warned about the troubling challenges we might face as an interracial couple—especially, he stressed, if we had children. Were we really prepared for this burden and difficulty? Was he sure this was worth it? It was 2004 and I was sixteen.

Any ideals I'd had about the separation of politics and religion were dissolved with 9/11 and their mutual cause-effect collusion over-apparent by the 2004 presidential race, which at my school was about abortion. There had been no attempt on the part of my teachers to mask their personal views, and no hesitation to present them as the views of the Church and the indisputable word of God. The secular world we'd been warned about was soon conflated with Democrats in fairly explicit terms, and irrelevant of their narrative context, biblical verses commanded present behavior and ideology.

Meanwhile, as religious rhetoric became more political, and conservative politicians more directly invoked "moral responsibility," the Republican Party reaped the benefits of an increasingly influential political voice with ever-evolving platforms and ever-growing constituencies, many with hateful agendas hidden under words like *family values* and *pro-life*, designed to Satanize the "threatening" liberal government. White pastors nationwide banded together to form the "Moral Majority" who would elect Ronald Reagan; the evangelical conservatives who would ardently back GWB's blindfolded attacks on Middle Eastern countries and sanctify hate crimes against Middle Eastern–colored Americans; the followers of "Christian Identity" who would demand President Obama's US birth certificate like a head on a stake.

In 2008, Bob Jones University released a "Statement About Race at BJU," apologizing for the "segregationist ethos" embraced "in its early stages," and admitting that, "Though no known antagonism toward minorities or expressions of racism on a personal level have ever been tolerated on our campus, we allowed institutional policies to remain in place that were racially hurtful." A slippery repackaging of its founder's words, the statement reiterates the university's commitment to "disregarding the economic, cultural and racial divisions invented by sinful humanity." And echoing the two-hundred-year-old *Christian Doctrine of Slavery*, the not-quite-apology underscores that "the true unity of humanity is found only through faith in Christ alone for salvation from sin—in contrast to the superficial unity found in humanistic philosophies or political points of view."

One spring Sunday in 2013, Pastor Donny Reagan of Happy Valley Church of Jesus Christ in Johnson City, Tennessee, lugged the "segregationist ethos" into a fresh decade, preaching, "What white woman would want her baby to be a mulatto by a colored man?" In the seventeen-minute, video-recorded sermon against biracial marriage (or "hybreeding"), he parrots Bob Jones Sr. almost word for word: "Some of the finest people I ever met in my life was some of them colored people." Fifty-nine years after the *Brown v. Board of Education* ruling, forty-eight years after the passage of the Voting Rights Act, more than a year into the second term of a Black presidency, even five years after Bob Jones University mea-culpa'd its most enduring belief, a white evangelical pastor ministered to a congregation of six hundred that, "If you do your mixing, you can't bring yourself back again." Bearing mixed-race children, he says, is "another defiance of God's law, it's a worldly way."

What's scary about the religious right is that it's not a religion. It's not a political party, either. But it's a force—and they know that. They helped bankroll our current president's campaign, prayed over him, planted his propaganda in church lawns.

Today, on record, our president says, "We take them out by the thousands. And they are monsters."

IN THEORY, MAYBE IT SEEMS REASONABLE TO FEAR THE INFIL-trating swarms of people demanding to be counted as such. In practice, do we not rely on the unwelcome, the Other, for their crucial roles in our comfortable, money-thirsty life-styles?

Where would Dr. Bob Jones and other racist white Christians be without the free Africans, the African Americans, who labored building their chapels, who chose nonviolence, who knew Scripture with equal but opposite clarity and read God's demand for acceptance?

Where would this president be without guys like Bob? Without the millions in campaign funding and political sup-port from the National Prayer Breakfast, and Focus on the Family and other white Christian organizations; the congre-gations praying for his safety and success; the immigrants who believe in his alarmist rhetoric; the assimilated children of immigrants who voted for him because they were told it was the Christian thing to do; the untaxed income from ne-glected properties and tenants, who rarely complain for fear of deportation or gentrification or any number of other methods of displacement; "the other half" that makes his privilege whole?

Where would he and other wealthy white Republicans

be without the immigrants who starch their shirts and wash their underwear; who prepare their food and who invented the cuisine; who populate their prisons; who obey their commercials and create their media; who enlist instead of their sons; who serve time in their stead; who teach their daughters to dance; who are the labor force and the consumer and the economy. Without all the "monsters" bringing in drugs to subsidize their bailouts and guns to arm their disciples, all the returns on investments in the slow or quick deaths of Other Americans? What if there had been a wall when their families arrived?

PASTOR BOB CLOSES THE SEGREGATION SERMON IN PRAYER: "Help these colored Christians not to get swept away by the propaganda . . . and to understand God's established order," and then some stuff about "thy glory," and then he actually says "Amen."

February 2019. Before the year is over, an interracial Christian couple in Mississippi will be dropped by their wedding venue, according to the owner, "Because of our Christian race—I mean, our Christian belief."

America has always called itself a *Christian nation*. We ask God to bless us every chance we get. Actually, it's more of a command.

WE IN THE MONEY

Part of the reason I subconsciously delay preparing and paying my taxes is how American currency began, which is also how I began.

To call it blood money would be too simplistic. That's why I'd prefer my reparations in another economic form, because American money is so low-down and dirty. Because it used to mean my body and my everything, down to the penny, and handing my own self back to me is not an apology nor an admission of guilt. It's a sick joke. You have to laugh.

At present writing, my personal net worth is in the negative six figures.

I wonder if there's a way to calculate if you're worth more dead than alive. I probably know the answer.

. . .

IN 1781, APPROXIMATELY FOUR HUNDRED AFRICAN PEOPLE WERE in transit, their souls lining the belly of a slave ship named *Zong*, when the vessel became low on water. The traders had been overeager, the crew had been greedy, and they piled on almost three hundred more slaves than they should have. People were dying, and slaves were dying, too.

Then they get lost, far off course with only enough water for a few more days, and much farther to go. To lighten the load and properly ration the water, the crew tossed more than 130 African people out of the boat and drowned them.

In 1781, hundreds of us caught in mid-Atlantic midair, still in space but already underwater—an opening, an ending, a frame of mind.

ONE THING I ALWAYS WONDER ABOUT THE UNITED STATES OF America Experiment is why there was so little foresight, truly shitty planning. The first obvious blunder is arriving at a "new" country—a land of people, but not yours, so not a country—and just murdering everybody. Second, having buried the only experts on the land and its bounties, and not realizing you'd have to work to sustain yourselves in this newly established place, your best idea is to go "buy" other humans from another continent to enslave and force them to earn your money. A comedy of errors ensues. You pat yourself on the back and have never felt so free.

Of course, everyone got insurance on their slaves. This

much seemed obvious. The bottom line is to protect the investment.

Because some of the "goods" being transported were thrown overboard in order to preserve the remaining cargo, rather than the entire shipment arriving dead of perfectly natural causes, or half dead for the same reasons, slave ship management filed a claim for their insurance company to reimburse them for the lost merchandise. After lengthy court proceedings—including the question of whether the crew should be tried for murder, seeing that the goods were, technically, souls as well—the slave trading company was reimbursed. For their losses.

On the first day went women and children. Next, the men. It rained that day. On the third day, some jumped as the crew tossed more asunder like wrong fish. On the fourth and fifth and sixth days, more. When the ship docked, there were thousands of liters of water leftover.

Maybe they considered it sacrifice. Christian, even. To this day, my country has an especially gut-wrenching and confounding way of theorizing a person, theorizing what is humane.

Ever since my transformation on the slave ship—my unbecoming, my skin made retail—my worth has been measured in my contribution to the bottom line. My penance for invading the bounds of habitation is unending. In all mixed communities, I am asked to explain myself, to come to my defense. *I am worth the trouble,* I plead with every word, *I make up for myself in value.* It is always about spinning peoples into moneys. Now, folded into American society, technically free and reluctantly allowed a place—unless I am earning my keep through entertainment or excessive labor—my African American body is an unrented apartment, sitting there with no return. Bleeding money.

I believe this is at the core of why I am so bad with money—the other reasons for which are also directly linked to the lingering effects of American slavery on a white supremacist capitalist economy, including but not limited to the lack of financial literacy education and accessibility for Black descendants of slaves, whose legitimacy of citizenship and personhood is enduringly murky, and for whom the American capitalist economy was never meant to be legible or useful.

I was the first person in my family to be able to graduate from college, the first to be unemployed on purpose, and maybe the second to (briefly) have more money than I know what to do with. To have money to do something with, other than give it back. In theory I'd like to be better with my money, to be even as economically literate as my white Ivy League peers were freshman year. In reality, even thinking about it makes me sick to my stomach.

Education, finance, the panopticons of prisons and projects and public schools—these are systems that do not consider me a person, or worthy of too much investment if any at all. The body and "assets" I will leave behind are still worth more than what's currently in my bank account. This is the truth stuck in the back of everybody's mind. How easily we become casualties.

Zong holds up miraculously as a template for the after-math of Hurricane Katrina, the carceral system, the crack epidemic, and the treatment of Black students. It serves as a model for a particularly chilly form of institutional neglect. The rationalizing, the distillation of matter into monetary.

ROBIN D. G. KELLEY WROTE THAT "THE HISTORY OF BLACK PEO-ple has been a history of movement—real and imagined." Kelley links Marcus Garvey's Black Star Line, in particular, to an economic ideology that recalls the philosophy of the Atlantic slave trade even as it rewrites it, a call to "economic independence and entrepreneurship."

In the 1920s, the ship was set to sail back to Africa—our promised land was our origin. For Garvey, escaping the slave ship meant turning it around. Kelley calls the Black Star Line a new ark, referencing Noah's ark in Genesis, and vi-sions of Africa, the Promised Land of Exodus.

But the continent of Africa can't stand in for an unknown utopia—it's too busy being the continent of Africa. Our ideo-logical journey to freedom is—perhaps must be—a mash-up, an invented art form merging Exodus and Genesis and space odyssey. "The ark has taken the form of a modern space ship, and the search for the New Land has become intergalactic." Enter Sun Ra.

> *If we came from nowhere here*
> *Why can't we go somewhere there?*

Afrofuturism tells us the way off the boat is up, through the outer space of imagination. "At the heart of Sun Ra's vision was the notion of alter/destiny," Kelley writes, "the idea that through the creation of new myths we have the power to redirect the future." Or, both are simultaneous.

Old Testament Kanye West's grave shift conjured a slave ship, dreamed a spaceship. *Joke's on you we're still alive.* New Testament Kanye West compares picking cotton to buying Alexander Wang. *And the white man get paid off all of that.* New Testament Kanye West grieves, strays, surrenders control. *I know that we the new slaves.*

If the spaceship is the boat, and the slave ship is the boat, it encompasses both the continual search for lost identity and the flexible resiliency of reinvention, both exit and return. Our promised land can be both our origin, and someplace new.

"Exodus provided Black people with a language," explains Kelley, "for its central theme wasn't simply escape but a new beginning. Exodus represented dreams of Black self-determination, of being on our own, under our own rules and beliefs, developing our own cultures, without interference." It's where we got "Back to Africa," Black Wall Street, Black Jesus, and Black Power. It's why my favorite holiday is Passover. Maybe it's why there are so many Black Moseses. Harriet Tubman, Garvey, *Black Moses* Isaac Hayes with a powder-blue gold-plated Cadillac for a ship. We embody the flexibility of resettlement. Odyssey and inheritance.

Sometimes I forget the whole story of Noah's ark. We

have a tendency to think about the animals, of course, and not why they were there: waiting out the end of the world. Dank, lonely nights in the ark's belly, waiting. How it might have felt to be the first goods aboard, the first holy beings transported over waters in order to be used, worked, consumed, bred, beaten, mimicked, worn, sold, certified, showboated, and house-trained. How without them, no new world would be necessary.

REPARATIONS (OR, STRATEGIES FOR BOAT REPAIR)

We'd need to agree on a definition of the word *reparations*. Whether we're talking about remuneration or repair, should these not be the same results. There are major differences; mainly that reimbursement requires follow-up action to achieve restoration. One is a payoff.

There are a host of decisions to be made, including who should be making them—and also who will be making them, should these not be the same persons.

There is the question of who pays and why. From whose means, and the meaning of their culpability. There is probably a question of how as in from where, as in which funds.

There is the specific question of why as in what for, which reasons.

There's the important question of how, as in through

what means of remittance, which demands further consideration of why as in for which damages incurred, which is above all, a very personal thing.

There is the problem of the requirement of admission. (This is not my problem.)

There are multiple steps to this, making repairs. Those who ascribe to linearity should think of them as in response to the past, present, and future. Reparations for the past, and for the past's impact on the present and future. There is, in short, a lot to make up for.

There's the less-discussed consideration of toward what outcome and answer. The topic of why as in toward what impact, for what meaning, as statement of what. We would need an agreed-upon goal.

What form and extent of repair can be achieved with a check? Without new parts, additional paid labor, expert advice? Remuneration of funds—backpay and dividends—is a means, they think, of leveling the ground below us. Like it all just sets back to zero. But there is no point unless you change the soil underfoot: the way the grounds are tended, who does the tending. Which must be a terrifying thought. Responsibility. The kind where you have to do something.

Beginning with those who organize diversity brown-bag lunches and representation panels and brag about their Black interns. For their part, those people could quit their jobs and generally leave Black people alone—read up on race theory and be humble. Maybe CEOs resign, boards of directors are wiped clean; maybe money changes hands. Maybe streets and tunnels change their names, maybe officers change their outfits for once. Maybe you pay taxes and we are relieved. Maybe we say what relief looks like.

It seems fundamentally incorrect that the individual complainant have no input as to the denomination of funds issued. A one-size-fits-all approach to reparations distribution only reinforces the myth of our singular slave-ship beginning and misunderstands their purpose. To repair people, not just a problem.

Systemic oppression attacks psychologically, economically, spiritually. It seeks to destroy all arenas of the social and physical self, fits itself to any necessary shape. How each aspect of its harm throbs in each of us, the particular injuries to which we are each attuned, is different. Deep ache is intimate.

There is the question of what hurts, which demands every answer is heard. Every ailment requires individual attention, which invites wider and deeper consideration of not only how as in by what means but who as in for which offenses. As in perpetrators, in absolution of whose debt owed. Which requires more consideration of how as in by what means of distribution and what approach. This demands that *how* be personal.

The whys and what fors are multitudinous, which means the hows and whos are infinite. It means a lot of people can chip in, for a lot of different reasons, and in a lot of different ways. It means any right answer about reparations is dependent upon what we each say. We decide.

That's the whole point of this thing, to get out from under what they've already decided about us, what they always already decide. It matters how we hurt. It matters that we even do. This time our diagnoses will not be rushed.

SOME SYMPTOMS, SOME MEMORIES THAT MAY OCCUR IN BLACK American DNA: never knowing your real name; always fearing death; being expected to prove to your government that you simply "matter"; never seeing yourself on television; if you do see yourself on television, you are dead or dying or a joke; fearing that, in the event of your death, your life will be analyzed with the most precise scrutiny; being presumed guilty; receiving less for more. And then, there is unrecognized trauma, what's nestled under the surface of our psyches. Little contagions untreated.

There is a part of me that is always back on the boat. In the fourth-grade classroom of my "predominantly white" Christian school, learning the metaphors of light and dark, or watching news coverage about the "justifiable," fatal shooting of someone who looks like me—over and over again. My African American experience is one of repetition and exhaustion. Revisionist white imaginings and images of my history—me—shape my mind, such that I wonder if my mind is mine at all.

I used to think something was wrong with me. Now I think depression is the most normal thing about me. It's fitting that I'm hardwired to consider, daily, in a pill or a handful of pills, the slipperiness of my mortality. To always be poised for an ending.

You start to get used to the state-sanctioned interruptions to your self-esteem—*New York Times* breaking news push notifications, the disrespectfully small number of convictions, Fourth of July celebrations, hollow Juneteenth emails from corporations. The number of days (901) between the signing of the Emancipation Proclamation and Juneteenth, when slaves in Texas were finally informed of their freedom. The number of restrictions attached to said freedom. The number of ways in which Juneteenth is a metaphor for contemporary Black American Life. You start to understand how your debasement is built into the fabric and law.

Then it gets personal: The average number of other Black friends my white friends have. The uncomfortably abundant number of white friends I have. The number of times I have, in the middle of sexual intercourse, realized I was in a *Jungle Fever* situation. The number of Black women (0) among sixteen contestants on *Top Chef*. I can't even casually watch *Top Chef*. I can't even fuck a white guy without, however momentarily or dissociatively, being haunted by our respective ancestors and the body memory of mine underneath his—the body memory of that shame and violation.

It builds.

A government official in blackface. A white woman tells me she knows how it feels. A Black child is killed. A white fifth-grade classmate apologizes to me for slavery. A Black seventh-grade classmate calls me an Oreo. A complete stranger in a hotel bar asks me, *Why do you have to make everything about race?* A white man at the hotel bar says he is saving an empty barstool, so my friend and I take turns sharing one, and no one ever claims the seat. A Black person is beaten to death by the police and there is video of it. The video plays on every channel all month, and no one is indicted.

There's that scene in *Malcolm X*, in the library, when he discovers that even our dictionary, our language, insists on our inherent evil.

There's the Miami police officer who, when asked why he shot an unarmed Black man, responded, "I don't know." There's Officer Mark Fuhrman, of the O. J. Simpson case, who once said of a suspect, "He was a nigger. He didn't belong."

Imagine the psychology of being displaced, from land and self and history. Imagine being not only unwelcome but disposable—conditionally tolerated but otherwise, waste. Imagine, too, that the psychology goes both ways.

"How can another cop walk free?" a white acquaintance writes on Twitter.

On Facebook somebody posts a poorly photoshopped graphic that reads: "I didn't own any slaves, you didn't pick any cotton, case closed!" Kids at school used to say stuff like that, back in the post-Rodney nineties when racism was over.

I didn't pick any cotton. But this argument assumes a dangerously limited definition of *slavery*, and a simplistic understanding of its effects. American slavery, the event, begat American white supremacy, a psychology. American slavery, the industry, continues to fill the pockets and fuel the egos of white Americans with a shameful amount of power and privilege.

People use those words a lot, so much that I hesitate to utilize them here, in case they no longer register meaning. What I'm talking about is "benefit of the doubt." The "reasonable explanation" "you seem like a good kid" thing I've seen afforded to white friends again and again.

I'm talking about who's in prison and who owns the prison. I'm talking about the kids at college never suspected of shoplifting or selling coke. I'm talking about the difference between getting let off with a warning and getting shot until you're dead.

"I would have fought back," boys in elementary school would say, turning toward my desk. "Why didn't the slaves just fight back?"

DR. JOY DEGRUY DEFINES POST-TRAUMATIC SLAVE SYNDROME AS a combination of 1) "multigenerational trauma together with continued oppression" and 2) "absence of opportunity to access the benefits available in the society." Several behaviors and patterns are associated with this syndrome. She groups them into the following three categories: vacant esteem, ever-present anger, and racist socialization.

DeGruy describes these inherited conditions as "*transgenerational adaptations* associated with the past traumas of slavery and ongoing oppression." The unbearable conditions of my ancestors' lives instilled in them habits and behaviors, "in order to survive the stifling effects of chattel slavery, effects which are evident today." Each generation taught the next so that they might live.

There are shelves and shelves of available scientific research on ancestral traumas and memories. The transference of pain so deep and experiences so damaging, that their devastation cannot be contained or processed in one generation. A Black person can feel this. A Black person can access the feeling of an ancestor if the conditions are so constant and familiar, if the same triggers seem to resurface in every interaction.

I could cite Du Bois or Fanon. I could quote Baldwin, Frederick Douglass, Sojourner Truth. I could summon Dr. Alvin F. Poussaint, who wrote that "Most psychiatrists and psychologists would agree that the Negro American suffers from a marred self-image, of varying degree, which critically affects his entire psychological being." Published in 1966 in the *Journal of the National Medical Association*, his article "The Negro American: His Self-Image and Integration" explained in-depth how all angles of American culture, from mass media to religion to "white is right"—especially without sufficient "counter sources to this negative evaluation"— develops in us "conscious or unconscious feelings of inferiority, self-doubt, and self-hatred."

At least one layer of what I feel, in my physical body and in the spirit of my subconscious, is the product and perpetuation of the effects of slavery. Infecting me with a sickness of paranoia and gloom, a mind that betrays me. Making us hate ourselves and one another. Making us kill ourselves and one another, distrust ourselves and one another. Every slur and funeral and mispronounced name is a violence. I'm less of a person every day. This is another definition of slavery. My body is the plantation. My mind is chained to the boat.

When I try to get out, I'm pulled back to the past. When I dare to be the center of my own story, I realize how many of the thoughts plaguing and blocking me aren't mine at all. Then somebody gets killed. Then I step outside and I am inundated with my ugliness and soon, I believe my own insignificance. When I try to see myself differently, the world keeps looking at me the same. This is not the work of my neuroses, this does not concern my clinical diagnoses, this is not me.

This here is a white supremacist long con, slow and unyielding, a reminder that my existence is always up for debate, my esteem always under siege. And that's how it's been since the slave ship.

DeGruy reasons: "If one traumatic experience can result in distorted attitudes, dysfunctional behaviors and unwanted consequences, this pattern is magnified exponentially" when the trauma is dismissed, diminished, or goes unacknowledged altogether. "America's and Americans' denial of their blatant racism and the attending atrocities committed throughout the nation's history has become pathological. Such denial has allowed this illness to fester for almost 400 years." Each generation teaches the next.

Sounding just like my current therapist talking about the childhood defenses contributing to my intimacy issues, DeGruy explains that most of these learned, self-protective behaviors, "ensured our survival at one time or another.

Some of them will inhibit our ability to survive and thrive today if they are not brought to light, examined, and where necessary, replaced with behaviors which promote and maximize our progress."

"Slavery required the creation of a particular kind of person," Grier and Cobbs explain in *Black Rage*. "The ideal slave had to be absolutely dependent and have a deep consciousness of personal inferiority."

Too often, our learned strategies, as African American descendants of slaves, require us to oblige the belief that we are subservient, to understand the psychology of the oppressor, forgive it, and live in spite of it. Too often our learned behaviors are focused on living *with* pain, preservation instead of potential. Too often, for too many decades, we have had to forgo living for not dying.

"Teachings so painstakingly applied do not disappear easily," the psychiatrists write. "But along with their scars, Black people have a secret. Their genius is that they have survived."

The trauma lives in my blood, inextricable from me and my lived experience. Glory, too. That part is almost harder to swallow, because of how many times I've forgotten it.

According to its authors' introduction, *Black Rage* was intended as "a clinical handbook illustrating certain unique aspects of psychotherapy with blacks," foremostly "that racist mistreatment must be echoed and underlined as a fact"—not a question. Step one: Affirm our grievances. Step two: Acknowledge our grief. Step three: Allow it. This can be the difficult part: allowing us to live with our rage, when it's read only as a pathology, not an environmental response; behavioral and not historical.

Examining data from their case studies, the psychologists report that "many individual blacks feel a desperate alone-ness not readily explained," highlighting a particular "sadness and intimacy with misery which has become characteristic of Black Americans." They discuss "the proneness of Black women to depressive, self-deprecatory attitudes," how "those Black people who succumb to social ambition find them-selves in a similar precarious psychological position," and a phenomenon they term the *Black norm*: "a suspiciousness of one's environment which is necessary for survival."

Manifestations of the *Black Norm* (cultural depression and antisocialism, paranoia and compulsive vigilance) while "normal devices for 'making it' in America" may resemble "a posture so close to paranoid thinking" that Black people can be easily misdiagnosed by the wrong therapist. Before a Black person can even be assessed as "a proper subject for therapeutic endeavor," they suggest, "one must first total all that appears to represent illness and subtract the Black Norm." One must first find out which pain came first and from where, what is borne and what is born into, what's been adapted and what's been inherited. "The gravest dan-ger we see," they write, "is that unscrupulous people may use psychotherapy with blacks as a means of social control, to persuade the patient to be satisfied with [their] lot." By its conceptual nature, by deeming some behaviors divergent from a "norm," therapy and psychiatry could be just another form of oppression and assimilation in the wrong hands. But in practice, if approached with intentional inquiries and end goals, it has the potential to settle our psyches beyond measure. To make us better as Black people, not just as American citizens. To give us some of ourselves back.

THERE ARE CAVEATS. WE WOULD NEED TO AGREE ON THE MEANing of the word *therapy*. We'd have to specifically decide to utilize it toward African American psychological liberation. There are logistical considerations, accompanying demands, and certainly additional expenses—such as educational and employment funds for Black psychiatrists, who know about double consciousness, who know our fears are valid and our loneliness makes sense, and can tell us so.

In a 1969 article calling for "Black teachers of Black studies," June Jordan explained, "It is not that we believe only Black people can understand the Black experience. It is, rather, that we acknowledge the difference between reality and criticism as the difference between the Host and the Parasite."

It isn't that Black people require more specialized treatment than any other group, or that our "pathology" is so far outside the scope of basic psychiatric skills—it's that we are outside the scope of psychiatry. Psychoanalysis as a practice is outside the scope of us and our experience, the *psych-* part of it. The formula itself has not considered alternate "familial" or cultural structures outside of the dominant European/Western tradition. Of course the practice can amend itself to address what is alternative to its European roots, but maybe it combusts in the face of a culture that its inventor has and indeed actively is trying to stamp out, overwrite with its own psychological coding.

Grier and Cobbs suggest a format that "bears some re-semblance to military psychiatry, where the psychiatrist must keep fit for duty the warrior whose primary function is to oppose the enemy." In order for Black Americans to live and flourish, "they must oppose racism in an unrelenting way. Psychiatry for such warriors aims to keep them fit for the duty at hand and healthy enough to enjoy the victories that are certain to come." The psychiatrist must be invested, actively, in the shared opposition to racism if they are to, as their job insists, be invested in their patient's certain vic-tory—as a Black person. They must understand a mind can-not be healthy without honest exploration of the forces it battles, internal and national. And they have to understand what those battles have required of us.

Warrior has always been a necessary verb, a useful defini-tion of how to get by in the absence of ceasefire. But I'm no longer satisfied with getting by. This is about getting out from under.

REFRAIN AND REFRAIN AND REFRAIN: JULY

In 2016, my therapist was a dope Asian woman with offices above an obnoxious yoga studio frequented by young, thin white women in Lululemon. Every two weeks on my lunch break, I stuffed my sulking self into the back of the tight lobby elevator to ride up the few floors with them smiling en route to their midday stretches with barely sipped $8.95 juices, as if nourishment were beside the point, and "wellness" were something one could "practice" and achieve.

I was in the "learn to love yourself so you can fall in love" phase of my therapy and my twenties. On my shelves in Brooklyn was a barely read book called *Inequalities of Love: College-Educated Black Women and the Barriers to Romance and Family*, and I had promised my therapist I was ready to finally confront my intimacy issues and make myself open and available to a relationship. It wasn't going well.

When I swore I was ready and looking, I'd been willing it, as if to conjure it true. Where was there to look? When I promised myself I was ready to "receive" love, I didn't trust that it would come find me where I wasn't looking, if I wasn't laboring to earn it.

By then, with a book under my belt and another in the proverbial oven, people had stopped asking me how I was doing. If I bumped into a poet or a Facebook friend from college, they either provided their condolences for the murder of an unarmed Black person, or greeted me with vague and unprompted congratulations. "Looks like you're doing so great! Kicking butt! Congrats!"

How and at what point in the conversation could I say otherwise? Who was I to tell them who they're talking about isn't *me* me? That this person smiling in front of them is the one getting her ass kicked, again and again, by every news alert and her own goddamn mind? The name on my book cover was starting to become another person, and I was beginning to despair, seeing how easily I could get lost. My therapist had been telling me that if I needed help, I should ask for it. That wasn't going phenomenally, either. Felt almost dangerous.

I liked this therapist a lot; she remains one of my favorites. She laughed at all my jokes, and then called me out on their defensive nature. In other words, she let me have my defenses and grow from them too, which I appreciated in spite of my stubbornness. In her office I could freely disparage white women's hold on everybody and everything, develop shorthand descriptions without much explanation, and confess my deep mistrust of linear time without judgment. Sometimes I cried in her office, which is to say I felt safe with her.

"I never stood a chance of loving myself," I sighed one day, truth like bile working its way to my throat. "Even allowing myself to be loved." (I'd been learning the two weren't interchangeable, that one didn't guarantee the other, and both were on our psychiatric agenda. Both kept getting delayed by the news and its too-present dangers.)

Across from me in an orange wingback chair, a few feet above the panic attack of Union Square, my therapist nodded in pity: She couldn't argue with me. Look at the ads in the subway, I pleaded. White women everywhere, flaunting everything I lacked. In all the ads for makeup or hair care products, fashion standards modeled on her figure, tailored for her measurements, and the color "nude" in her image; in all the ads for the dating site—advertising, quite literally, love and beauty. This is old information by now, but still, we let it keep happening, and still, I'm supposed to pretend it doesn't hurt, doesn't dare me to hate myself.

At twenty-eight, I felt defeated by the brick barriers to protected aliveness and even casual sex. Until then, I'd thought "love" more improbable than unequal. "Romance and family"? Much too big of an ask.

For years by then, a scientific research article had been floating around the internet, reporting that according to empirical data, the least desirable group on dating apps is Black women. We're not the ones anyone's looking for, not the pictures that jump out like centerfolds. According to empirical data, my pictures either repel or don't register as viable. Love and romance seemed just another thing, like impromptu soul-searching in Bali, marketed for American women but only applicable to American women without hyphens. I was starting to worry that love and romance were my sacrifice for being myself.

I was bitter, and I hated how bitter I was. It was starting to eat me from inside. I didn't realize, at the time, it was fear. Anything I did could be the wrong move; anything, I felt, could be fatal. I couldn't stop thinking it. It was more than garden-variety fear of dying alone; it was also the fear that I was supposed to, that I deserved it.

My thing about white girls is in fact a matter of the politics of ego development. Insomuch as we, the fiction of African American people as conceptualized by "America," exist under the political and therefore social category only as an Other—only in relation to whiteness, a mirror and contrast, a categorical invention of the colonizer. Because we the Black people in our Blackness are people. Insomuch as whitegirlness has harmed my Blackgirlness, it is my enemy, it has done harm to my Self as a Black Woman and thus must be relentlessly interrogated and destructed if I am to attain the freedom to self-determine—and yeah, find good, true love—so the bitterness and mounding rage, the scoffs and eye cuts I can't hold in, don't really have shit to do with them, so much as my loneliness to defend, my pain to express, my right to hunt what haunts me. My thing about white girls is a matter of private torment and a matter of public safety and these facts accompany the larger problem.

The truth is, I was beginning to love myself—both the self the public loved and the one I didn't let them see. When I said I hated myself, I'd only been reciting a script, which by then I knew was fiction. The truth was that self-love didn't matter, and self-care was usurped by warfare, and Sandra was still dead. They'd still ruled it suicide. Even if our lives mattered, they were worth far less than anyone else's, whether walking around or in the ground.

Police killings raged on, hotly ignited by election rhetoric and failure of justice for the hundreds of unarmed Black people slain by police in the too-recent past. For at least two years, Trayvon Martin's murderer, George Zimmerman, a self-declared "neighborhood watch" citizen and self-appointed, self-corrupted law enforcer, had been making substantial money on appearances and autograph signings at gun shows across the nation. To stand one's ground was to rip somebody else's from under them. It was starting to feel dangerous not to be suspicious.

July was hell. It was the worst Fifth of July since Frederick Douglass was invited to give a speech at an "Independence Day Celebration" in Rochester—more than ten years before the Emancipation Proclamation. "Why am I called upon to speak today?" he asked. "Do you mean, citizens, to mock me?"

That year, I started my annual tradition of reading his speech aloud, taking my time with it, consuming it whole instead of in Instagramable quotations. Some lines I read a second or third time, with increasing fervor or frustration or familiarity. *Do you mean to mock me?* As years and murders went on, I'd begin sending the PDF as response to unrelated emails. "This Fourth of July is *yours*," Douglass said, "not *mine*. *You* may rejoice, *I* must mourn."

July 5, 2016, Baton Rouge, Louisiana. Alton Sterling is murdered by two white police officers during a ninety-second altercation recorded by multiple bystanders. Though he'd been pinned to the asphalt, under their knees, under the weight of their rage or fear or both, police claimed that as they attempted to "control" Sterling for *resisting* (by then, we knew this word to mean "existing"), they witnessed him reach for a loaded .38 caliber handgun. The video went viral. You've seen it. Whoever you are, you've seen it by now.

That next day, another video and another slaying, this time during a routine traffic stop in Saint Paul, Minnesota, with the victim's girlfriend and her four-year-old daughter in the back seat. Dashcam footage shows Officer Jeronimo Yanez pulling over thirty-two-year-old Philando Castile for a busted brake light. If you blinked, you'd miss it. Sudden, rapid gunfire. Seven panicked shots into the vehicle. Then he's dead, just like that. *Fuck fuck fuck fuck fuck*, Yanez is heard saying after the slaughter. "I was getting fucking nervous!" he recounts in a grainy dashcam video to a backup officer who pats his shoulder reassuringly, like it's the end of a damn *Law & Order* episode. Like Yanez hadn't willingly and eagerly endangered a toddler and impulsively executed a thirty-two-year-old man—seven shots in rapid succession—and he was the one who needed soothing.

Later that same night, more footage of Alton's murder was released, on loop on every channel, and the owner of the convenience store where it had taken place told NBC News that Sterling, known to locals as the "CD man," hadn't threatened anyone and never wielded a gun at the scene.

We'd suspected as much, about all of it, but we hated to admit that somehow it hurt more, so blatantly out in public, on record, official and provable; because that made not one lick of difference, except sometimes, it wasn't even safe to watch TV.

I think often about Walter Benjamin's essay "The Work of Art in the Age of Mechanical Reproduction," from the turn of the twentieth century, wherein Benjamin discusses how the new technologies of photography and film threatened to disrupt our perceptions and corrode our sense of original self. There is a disturbance in the power structure between object and creator, spectator and actor. My dude Benjamin could not have predicted how much corrosion the self would endure, how soon we would willingly sell our perceptions. We are post-shock, beyond disruption. We absorb everything—especially our beliefs—without noticing.

It is not random. I grew up sixty miles from LA, and though I was too young to fully comprehend the Rodney King beating, the video was inescapable and impacted every one of my young instincts. It was my first lesson of the fiction of protection. Now, after years of cross-culturally normalizing video as a primary mode of communication and entertainment, footage of the murders of Black people regularly inundates the news, triggers be damned. There is no

escaping death—Look! Boom you're dead—there is no escaping the brutal possibility of this—Look again! See it!
Look!—this insignificant and purposeless death. *Viral.*

THERE WERE THOSE TWO DAYS IN A ROW, AND THEN FOR BLACK
people, there were all the nights that followed, when new
grief was always waiting, just around the corner, like hot
breath on our necks. It got to be you were afraid to open
your eyes in the morning, just in case there was more news.
I already faced the daily challenge of racing my depression
out of bed.

When the FBI and law enforcement didn't, *The Guardian* launched "The Counted" to track the numbers and collect data. To document stories. Most of the evidence, though,
was caught on camera. Most of the murders went unavenged,
most officers eventually forgiven.

In more than eighty instances of police violence that year,
"the initial contact with law enforcement began following a
call reporting that the person was suicidal or harming themselves, or attempting to harm themselves." According to *The
Guardian's* reports, at least one in five people killed by police
in 2016 was mentally ill or in the midst of a mental health
crisis at the time—and the risk of being killed by police is at
least sixteen times greater for people with mental illness.

The Washington Post reports that 958 people were killed
by the police in 2016; of these, 248 were reported to have a
mental illness—which is roughly a quarter. Many were armed
and dangerous to themselves, but the cops are trained to see

the armed part, they are trained to ignore the second part, and if they're responding to a call of someone threatening to kill themselves, maybe they hear it as an invitation, even a task. I don't know the details about police training. I know, if I am feeling suicidal, dangerous to myself and in possession of say a kitchen knife, because I don't keep guns in my house for this reason, if I am experiencing a true mental health crisis, I would not call the police. I don't know who I'd call. Every therapist's voicemail says call 911 if it's an emergency.

And what if I had hallucinations brought on by a new medication, paranoia, anger, any number of potential side effects? If I displayed a "combative stance"—as with mentally ill Joseph Mann, fifty, killed that July for "acting erratically"; or my anxiety read as suspicious—as with mentally ill thirty-eight-year-old Alfred Olango, whose removal of a vape from his pocket looked like "a shooting stance" to the El Cajon police responding to reports of a man "behaving erratically," proved instantaneously fatal that September? What if I was behaving erratically, according to someone, for any number of reasons, and what exactly does that mean? (Am I doing it right now?)

There are too many variables, and the guns introduce a particularly dangerous one. There are just so many guns and every minute could be fatal.

Of course, I wouldn't call the police if I got into a fender bender. No one is trained to believe me. Procedure is to approach us with suspicion. I don't expect anyone to want to help me, and they don't expect to need to.

Most of the dashcam evidence is from routine traffic stops that end up with cops saying things like "Basically, the fight was on." There is even more danger for me. They could say I hanged myself in a holding cell.

They could say, and it would be true, that I was suicidal, and that would make my death even more excusable. If they think like this, I have to think like this. If we are talking real dollars and cents, at face value, I'm easily extinguishable, "no human involved."

Most cops don't have mental health training, maybe even no experience with mental illness, maybe even no experience with a Black person, but they have suspicions, and guns. They have been armed intentionally with suspicion and guns and no training. They are not from the neighborhood and they don't talk to the neighbors and they don't know "he was just a little slow" or living with schizophrenia, or as in several fatal cases, mere days out of a mental health treatment facility.

That officers are virtually untrained; that they have far more guns than hands and sticky hands when they don't know what to do; that nobody shoots to maim anymore; that they are trained to fear and abolish anything "not right" or "out of the ordinary" and then reminded once again about the handy guns—this is more than an oversight. It's criminally negligent and ethically despicable, a breach of contract to protect.

Sometimes I think about that word, *protection*—all the definitions we might be inferring when using it. I think over its syllables and senses as if writing a poem: What would protection feel like? What should it? What is the actual meaning of the word, if we have gotten it so wrong, so faith-fully?

IN 2012—SOON AFTER TRAYVON'S DEATH AND BEFORE HIS KILLER went unpunished—a sixty-two-year-old Bronx woman named Deborah Danner wrote an essay, "Living with Schizophrenia," about her experiences and fears as a mentally ill woman—in treatment, on medication, supported by family—but still mentally ill and Black. She writes about how stigma and igno-rance can be fatal for incarcerated, homeless, and undiagnosed mentally ill people and "the all too frequent news stories about the mentally ill who come up against law enforcement in-stead of mental health professionals and end up dead."

She tells the story of another New York woman whose mental health crisis was "perceived as 'a threat to the safety' of several grown men who were also police officers," who chose to subdue her by using deadly force. With bullet points and graphs, she pleads for police training: methodolo-gies for diagnosing and treating those at risk for mental ill-nesses. She demands, "the homeless mentally ill have to be housed and treated, somehow" (almost admitting the sad unlikelihood)—"a wish list of mine that I generated during a period of reflection on the plight of [others] like me."

Deborah has learned to be good with her words—emphatic, specific, impassioned, effective, loud—because she has not been heard. "Living with Schizophrenia" has been for her, "not only a curse but oftentimes a nightmare." She'd lost jobs and relationships, battled overwhelming stigma, and felt haunted by flashbacks of her darkest moments, even visions of the knife she'd carried intending to kill herself. She writes on behalf of those moments, of her own anger and, yes, misery—because she wants everyone to survive as she has, because the devastating part is that there are solutions.

By the end of 2016 Deborah Danner was dead. Fatally shot in her home within five minutes by an NYPD sergeant, whose lethal force was deemed "entirely consistent with good police tactics."

This is a chorus heard over and over.

Upon their entry into her apartment, police witnessed Deborah picking up a baseball bat, which is not a surprising reaction from a senior citizen living with schizophrenia, nor a threatening one, but it had been enough to put her blood on her own hands. The officers had been responding to reports of an "emotionally disturbed person" and found her holding a pair of scissors, completely naked. She was sixty-six.

WHAT IS TO LOVE ABOUT THIS BODY I'M IN, THIS MIND I'M stuck with, too? I have wanted to kill myself. I have accepted this, and apologized to myself for it, forgiven it, and yet, I can't psychologically accept that authorities also want to kill me. It would be simple and reasonable for armed authorities to heed the extra encouragement. Like they did with Ezell. Like they did that July with Joseph Mann, or that May with Ronald D. Williams, who'd been threatening to harm himself, or that March in Florida, when sixteen-year-old Robert Dentmond had himself called to tell 911 dispatchers he had a gun and wanted to kill himself.

It had been a toy gun, officers discovered when it was too late for them to pretend to care. Maybe Dentmond had thought if he said so, they wouldn't take his cry for help seriously. That if the gun weren't real, the urgency of his pain wouldn't be, either. And I often wonder how many days and nights and how much courage it must have taken a sixteen-year-old Black boy to admit he was suicidal, how many times he must have been dismissed before.

Just ten days earlier, twenty-two-year-old Arteair Porter Jr. had done the same thing, called Reno police and confessed he was suicidal and holding a weapon, pointed it at responding officers who didn't bother to find out before killing him without hesitation or consequence that it was a toy gun. No psychiatrist or mental health worker had arrived on the scene of the armed and suicidal young man, yet officers from several local and neighboring departments showed up and opened fire.

"Suicide by cop" is a thing in this country. Still every year I owe taxes for my assured protection, which I was made to believe—and which they keep telling me—includes protection from myself.

I can't accept that there is nowhere to call in case of emergency, that everywhere outside my body, I'm wished dead, too. It would be too dangerous to see the danger everywhere it could be. So I can't think about it that way. I am begging to be shown another way.

Could it be that if I ask for death—whether in my right mind or not, whether under duress or under the influence, whether psychologically sound enough to make such a choice, whether or not I might change my mind or could be encouraged otherwise—I deserve it?

I have been working on this book for four years now. It has been five years since Michael Brown's murderer was cleared of charges by the United States Department of Justice and the grand jury of his peers. It has been six years since Michael Brown raised his hands while the officer fired twelve bullets, which was a month after Eric Garner's eleven pleas of I can't breathe did nothing to stop the NYPD from choking him to death right on camera in public, without consequences. It's been nine midnights since Breonna Taylor was startled from sleep and murdered by plainclothes officers in her own home. It's been fifty-one years since Fred Hampton laid down next to his pregnant fiancée on an unbloodied mattress and was assassinated by the Chicago police before dawn. It's been eight years since the wave of protests against the monster who killed a child *named Trayvon, six since a baby named Tamir was playing in the park and gunned down by the local police before dusk. I think I'm gonna stop writing this.*

O! TWENTY-EIGHT YEARS SINCE LAPD BEAT THE EVER-LIVING SHIT out of Rodney King—remember how it was so shocking? "Disturbing footage." "Hard to watch." For twenty-eight years it has been my job to understand the Rodney King footage, the look in their eyes. Isn't it shocking now—to see he lived? Isn't it weird how much easier it gets to watch? For twenty-eight years it has been my job to say, explain, convince, prove that I do not deserve this beating, so I think I will just stop writing this essay. White people everywhere still do not have TVs, do not involve themselves with the noise in the parks below their doorman apartments, do not understand what I am talking about.

Once I was young, tucking a rose quartz into my left bra cup to balance the internalized self-hatred I had finally come to understand as an extension of the white supremacist ideologies permeating and governing the nation of which I am a citizen. I endeavored to write an essay about therapy and reparations, how the government should reimburse me for years of sessions devoted to the country's problems, with mine only secondary, mine always pointing back to theirs. A source beyond me, blockages that existed long before me and my neuroses. About how, with the constant debate over my worthiness, constant threat of "routine" murder—the constant routine of grief and protest, grief and resignation—it was impossible to move forward. About how for years I'd been working hard and paying greatly, in emotional distress and by check, to close wounds and heal myself, my progress always sabotaged by the white supremacist fibers of my country—both in my head and out in the world.

I believed words could be the pathway to empathy and writing an active resistance against hate. A fool! Now I know language is the war; that language lets "killing of Black person [Certified Human Deserving of Life] by officer [employed to protect said person]" grow into "officer-involved shooting." I write in defense of language and with the defense of language. I write to communicate such that the reader might experience the slightest shift of understanding or emotion. I wrote and have written instead of marching or lying down to risk my Black life and sanity, this very Black life in question, and look where we are. I have failed at my job and so I am no longer writing this. Reader, I should have finished this book years ago. I don't even wanna talk about this anymore.

CHEAPER THAN THERAPY

I first pitched the free therapy idea to my friend over wine on a patio in Bed-Stuy. Gesturing toward the speakers eking out "Flashing Lights," I said, "Imagine what Kanye could make if he weren't ill! Imagine what we could make." Personally, I'm already doing a phenomenal job, and I'm entirely swallowed by centuries of fear and trauma. Imagine not having all these cards against us. My friend smiled, and I deflated the more I thought about it, the more I listened to Kanye—proclaiming to hate paparazzi more than Nazis, his memory's museum, the both poignant and regular descriptions of loneliness as "like Katrina with no FEMA" and "Martin with no Gina"—I thought of all the music we've made, all the unimaginable lives we've lived, all our mastery.

Already by then, in 2016, Kanye's pain and confusion

had displayed itself in worrisome ways. Publicly there had been no diagnosis, but I worried about his mind, not just in the sense of tabloid celebrity schadenfreude. I marveled at his mind. The combination of glory and predestined tragedy that Kanye West embodied became synonymous with our grief—that unique kind of Black grief laced with regret, admiration, sometimes pride, and head-hanging shame at a nation that preys on its visionaries, a world that won't let art grow on its own, with just a little water and light.

"But you know they'd never do that," I shrugged. The US government would never fund our healing. "They want us like this." Vulnerable, pliable. Impoverished or imprisoned by one symptom or another.

Plus, it would be expensive. That week alone, I'd paid my therapist $1,800 for several months of talk therapy, and $92 at Walgreens for one of the daily medications prescribed by my psychiatrist. My parents and I have spent tens of thousands of dollars over the years—it would probably turn my stomach to calculate the damage, maybe shock me into catatonia. If you tally the cost of each and every session, the hundreds of months of medication refills—at the generic price, not even name brand, and even after insurance coverage—the amount would surely pay all my back taxes, if not credit card debts as well.

People in cults are always saying *I figured it was cheaper than therapy!* in their post-escape documentaries, saying how anyone could've fallen into their situation, because *Isn't everyone looking for something at one point in their life?* But of course this is post-Reagan America, where you get what you pay for, and you don't have to work hard if you work smart. Skipping steps is a symbol of status.

In the long run, bypassing the cult thing and going straight to therapy would have been much cheaper. This is how much we stigmatize therapy. We would rather join a cult. We are not opposed to *healing*. We like the sound of that. Of being healed. We prefer the sound of *reparations* to the sound of sweaty, laborious *repairing*.

Any reparations package thus far presented would cost less than covering my therapy for even just the past ten years, wherein my country's plight has been the primary topic, but this is typical of the government, just like most people who say things are cheaper than therapy, who want to solve the problem without naming it. Who want erasure, total cure, instead of tools for mending and tending. Therapy is hard—but anything cheaper than therapy wouldn't be enough. Would be beside the point. Would invalidate our pain all over again.

As long as I want to be self-possessed and manageable—both for myself and to the government—this is an expense I will always have.

MY FRIEND IS ALSO A BLACK WRITER. WE'D BEEN TALKING ABOUT pain. We lived two blocks from each other then and, on the rare occasions that we saw each other, we'd always say, "Why don't we see each other more often?" This is how writer types are, and this is typical young-professional-in–New York. It's how things work when you're hustling. After long hours writing and editing at a major news media website, my friend was editing an unprofitable but brilliant Black literary magazine on the side. Who knows what combination of barely paying gigs I was pouring too much energy into those days. I just know it was too much, because I had nothing left for me.

Also, we were both raised to be isolated, to labor for our freedom. Each of us the brown of our SoCal classrooms, modeling excellence, working three times as hard, being good. These are the roles we have always played, and the fabric of society depends on the fulfillment of this assignment.

I am tired of surviving. I want to be relieved of the expectation of my sacrifice. I want to know who I could be in my right mind. I want us all to be able to imagine triumph.

My case for therapy as reparations is not a case so much as an ethic. While I haven't crunched the numbers or anything, which I know is the first thing on America's mind, I believe it's a more-than-fair proposition of remuneration for one of the grossest violations of human rights in the history of time, and how it provided "the foundation for the world's wealthiest nation." How it's provided millions of consumers and entertainers and patients and inmates. Our poor mental health keeps the whole thing running. Prisons and bail bonds, sports leagues, "retail therapy," big pharma, street pharma, police budgets, loan finance. Who gets paid if we get well?

If we are to define reparations as compensation for damages wrought from the most underlying and unrelenting effects of US slavery and systemic white supremacy—the root to examine is the part that shapes how we think. Even before the economic damage can be assessed, we have to recognize the repercussions of a psychology that would justify the event of American slavery in the first place, and how the continued dominance of that psychology renders any other solutions effectively useless anyway.

If we are to consider reparations for slavery to be repayment for wages lost from centuries of unpaid labor/indenture/torture; recoupment for lives lost and continued, state-sanctioned emotional distress; as well as the wages that may have been earned in years since, were it not for the psychological, political, and economic effects of slavery—then free our minds.

If we are to consider reparations an earnest and genuine effort to balance the scales of well-being and success unavailable to Black people in America as a result of the horrific enslavement of our people, made possible by white supremacy, which is itself a psychological aberration not yet extinguished, we all need therapy.

Therapy, as in, the opportunity to see our actions and impulses for what they are and from where they sprouted. Through whatever methods psychological or spiritual, before any equality can be rightly established in this nation, every citizen must confront their delusions. Baldwin told us, "Nothing can be changed until it is faced." There are two neuroses that I consider particularly American: the commitment to forgetting, and the inability to imagine what has not been. We are afraid even to imagine our own rehabilitation.

We have fooled ourselves into refusing to even imagine other ways, as if we ourselves, the ground we stand on, would vanish if we decided to start from scratch. Because it would. Because the land is stolen. Because bodies wash up.

ON ANOTHER BAR PATIO IN BROOKLYN, I PRESENT MY CAMPAIGN to a longtime friend, a white Jewish woman from college. She counters by asking (theoretically, she thinks) what I would write about, if I were healed of the past, released from the present-ness of it. What could I write about if not the effects of over four hundred years of literal and psychological enslavement, its consequences to my mental health and contribution to my daily fears and woes—including the unprecedented possibility of me declining another round? I hear: What if I wouldn't be the same person without my pain? What if I am my pain, and trauma is what makes my life a life?

Once, hanging out at someone's house, a white poet expressed jealousy of a gay Black poet's success, told me they wished they had so much material. Honestly I had no idea what to say.

I will not be grateful for my trauma. I will not believe my art depends on my trauma. I will not believe my art is suffering. I will not believe suffering is my personality. I will not be grateful for the guts of my material. I do not want pity. I will not call my trauma a gift, a leg up, or a consolation. I will not be fooled into using language of exploitation. I am not selling myself to you. I will not thank my oppressor. I do not need the pain of others to make art. I do not need to be hunted to create. I don't need another child to die to have something to say. I don't need this bullshit to untangle. I'm a fucking genius.

My college therapist once told me that every neuroses and blockage could be traced to a locus of fear. She would ask me again and again, "What is the fear?" Though I never liked my answers, which usually alternated between "death" and "abandonment," I became obsessed with asking the question. For white police officers who commit unjustified murder, for white politicians and heads of television networks or publishing houses or universities who—though they admit their inefficacy in protecting and promoting and celebrating people of color—do not step down from their posts, the answer, always, is relinquishing control.

What is the fear? I want to ask America. What, specifically, is terrifying about having a little less power, a little less clemency and esteem? Is it because you have assumed all these years we are savages whose nature is violent; because when we say we want justice, you assume we mean revenge? Is it that you worry we will treat you how you have treated us?

While you are busy fearing imagined riots, we are still not free. Refusing to admit that it was your knuckles that left the bruise doesn't make it less purple. The damage cannot be undone, lessened—it's too late for that. I'll be in therapy next week, and the week after, and no matter who is president, and even in the unlikely event that white supremacist systems are dismantled in my lifetime. The damage transcends poverty, policy, education, media, bloodshed.

The damage transcends whatever it is you call *time*. America, I don't want your filthy dollars. I want you to see me. I want you to let me see myself.

We are owed treatment for every neuroses handed down, pushed down our throats without consent. We are owed, if not an apology, silence when we speak. We are owed mental well-being and untainted self-understanding. A chance in hell. This investment in our minds is a matter of public health, a matter of human rights, and we are worth it.

We have never been free, in that we have never been allowed to define freedom for ourselves. We have never been fearless, in that we have always understood ourselves as a thing to fear. When we love ourselves, it is not a predisposition—it's a revolution.

The poet who was envious of another's plight—I think we were meant to understand that if he had the same "material," his poems might be better than the other's, even as good or as acclaimed—which can only mean he was joking, right? You can't take another person's powers, even if you take their body. This poetry we make from our own ashes and myths is an art of survival. And glory, too.

Acknowledgments

Many thanks to the editors of the publications where versions of the following essays first appeared:

"Watch Her Rise & Reign": ESPN, as "Rise & Reign: Growing Up in the Light of Serena Williams."

"National Emergencies": *Fight of the Century: Writers Reflect on 100 Years of Landmark ACLU Cases* (Simon & Schuster, 2020), as "Bob Jones Builds a Wall."

"Self Help": *Sex and the Single Woman: 24 Writers Reimagine Helen Gurley Brown's Cult Classic* (HarperCollins, 2022).

"George Bush Doesn't Care About Black People": *New York* magazine's *The Cut*, as "I Think About This a Lot: Kanye West at the Katrina Telethon."

"Are We Not Entertained?": *LennyLetter.*

Several essays contain excerpts from "How to Stay Sane While Black," published in *The New York Times* on November 20, 2016.

This book would never have been written if not for the incredible team of colleagues, friends, family, and therapists who've helped me over the last five years, including through a cross-country move, long stints of writer's block, and a global pandemic.

Thanks to my agent, Dan Kirschen, for championing this book from inception to last-minute indecision, and for pushing me, comforting me, and encouraging me with so much care. Thank you to my generous, attentive, thoughtful editor, Nicole Counts, for giving me the space I needed to dream this up, the support I needed to write it, and all the patience and grace I needed to finish it. Thank you to Chris, Carla, Oma, Tiffani, Avideh, and the rest of the insightful team at One World for their help and hard work shaping and making this book.

Thanks to the Casa Ecco Fellowship for providing time and space to work on these essays, and to Meg and Aria for their sisterhood.

Thank you to Tina Dubois, Christine Larusso, SA Smythe, Tommy Pico, Charif Shanahan, and Leah Feuer, for generously reading drafts of this manuscript and also listening to me complain about drafts of this manuscript.

Extremely humble thanks to Mom and Dad, Thomas Parker, Wendy Ashley, Clea Litewka, Angel Nafis, the Husbands, Vivian Lee, Saeed Jones, Nick Zaharapoulos, and the rest of the team "lowercase MP," named and unnamed, who continue to support and love not only the writing but the writer, who keep me inspired and keep me living.

Finally, thank you so much to my readers, who keep me writing.

ABOUT THE AUTHOR

Morgan Parker is a poet, essayist, and novelist. She is the author of the young adult novel *Who Put This Song On?* and the poetry collections *Other People's Comfort Keeps Me Up at Night, There Are More Beautiful Things Than Beyoncé,* and *Magical Negro,* which won the National Book Critics Circle Award. Recipient of a National Endowment for the Arts Literature Fellowship and winner of a Pushcart Prize, Parker has been hailed by *The New York Times* as "a dynamic craftsperson" and her work of "considerable consequence to American poetry." She received her bachelors in anthropology and creative writing from Columbia University and her MFA in poetry from NYU. Parker is a Cave Canem graduate fellow and co-curates the Poets with Attitude (PWA) reading series with Tommy Pico. With Angel Nafis, she is The Other Black Girl Collective. She lives in Los Angeles with her dog, Shirley.

morgan-parker.com
Twitter: @morganapple
Instagram: @morganapple0